Contents

About the Author

Dr Kerry Young has been involved in youth work since 1977 as a detached youth worker and national officer at the National Youth Bureau, National Association of Youth Clubs and The National Youth Agency.

She is now an independent consultant, researcher and writer at Harrington Young (Organisation Development Consultants).

You can contact her at kerry@harringtonyoung.co.uk

Acknowledgements

With thanks to De Montfort University

This book could not have been produced without the time, commitment and support of a huge number of people.

The 32 youth workers and young people who allowed themselves to be interviewed and who shared their thinking and experiences with warmth, openness, honesty and integrity.

Dr Neil Kendra, Yvonne Field and Amanda Harrington whose time, patience and invaluable comments helped to create the first edition of this book. John Pitts and Geoffrey Mann for their comments on early drafts of this second edition.

The National Youth Agency for allowing me to use interview material I had originally produced for the report on the 1996–99 Youth Work Development Grants Programme (Hunter et al., 1999).

Geoff Appleton for the cover design.

Thank you.

Contributors

Imran Ali
Lisa Allen
Mohinder Bagry
Neil Bevan
Hannah Buddle
Daniel Carmel-Brown
Michael Clarke
Kevin Crawford
Andrew Duncan
Jeremy Fishman
Teresa Geraghty
Abdul Ghaffar
Bushra Habib
Mo Hand
Paul Jennings
Ella Jess

Jennie Lamb
Paul Mattis
Kevin Murphy
Shamsi Rashid
Meurig Roberts
Ann Robinson
John Rose
Joy Scott-Thompson
Sangeeta Soni
Dave Stannard
Shahid Sultan
Courtney Taylor
Neal Terry
Myra Topper
Ricki Vigon
Jamie Weinrich

Please note: The perspectives offered and observations made are strictly the personal opinion of the individuals involved. As such, they do not necessarily represent the policy or position of any youth and community service or voluntary organisation by whom the individual may be employed.

Chapter 1

Introduction

Things change. There was a time when talk about youth work was conducted by way of vague references to relationships and processes; a time when the work was shrouded in a kind of precious veil. That is no longer possible and actually, never should have been, not if we were ever serious about supporting young people to reach their full potential or other such time honoured youth work aspirations. But anyway, that time has passed. Now, youth work has to be 'curriculum based', and it must produce recorded and accredited outcomes.

In some ways that is OK if by 'curriculum' we mean youth workers and young people having a clear sense of what is to be achieved (in terms of the benefits and learning gains for young people), the processes to be used and the measures by which workers and young people will be able to judge progress and achievements; and if by outcomes we mean the sort of personal and social development that equips young people with the knowledge, skills and dispositions to make informed decisions and take charge of their lives.

It also seems fine to expect that young people should be enabled and supported to be healthy, stay safe, enjoy and achieve, make a positive contribution and achieve economic well-being (DfES, 2003); and good news that services should:

- Be more responsive to what young people and their parents want.
- Balance greater opportunities and support with promoting young people's responsibilities.
- Be more integrated, efficient and effective.
- Improve outcomes for young people while narrowing the gap between those who do well and those who do not.
- Involve a wide range of organisations from the voluntary, community and private sectors in order to increase choice and secure the best outcomes.
- Build on the best of what is currently provided. (DfES, 2005)

All of this supports the 'Change for Children' agenda. But what is the youth work contribution to this and is it different from the contribution to be made by other forms of work with young people? In other words, does youth work have a particular contribution to make to young people's lives and is there a clear set of 'defining characteristics' that mark it off from other forms of work with young people that may target such issues as crime and anti-social behaviour, drugs and alcohol, young pregnancy, formal education, employment or training, community cohesion, or neighbourhood regeneration?

It has been suggested that seven 'defining features' *when configured together* produce the distinctive practice of youth work. Specifically, an explicit commitment to:

• Young people's voluntary participation.
• Seeking to tip balances of power in their favour.
• Responding to their expectation that youth work will offer them relaxation and fun.
• Responding to their expectation that youth work will penetrate unstimulating environments and break cycles of boredom by offering new experiences and challenging activities.
• Seeing and responding to them simply as young people, as untouched as possible by pre-set labels.
• Working on and from their 'territory', at times defined literally but also as appropriate to include their interests, their current activities and styles and their emotional concerns.
• Respecting and working through their peer networks. (Davies, 2005: 22)

Elsewhere, the 'key dimensions' of youth work have been defined as:

• Focusing on young people in the sense of being an age specific activity.
• Emphasising voluntary participation and relationship in the sense that young people freely enter into relationships with workers and end those relationships when they choose; and where relationships are seen as a fundamental source of learning.
• Committing to association in the sense of joining together in companionship or to undertake some task, and the educative power of playing one's part in a group or association.
• Being friendly and informal, and acting with integrity in the sense that workers should be approachable and friendly; have faith in people; and be trying, themselves, to live good lives. That youth work is driven by conversation and an evolving idea of what might make for well-being and growth.
• Being concerned with the education and, more broadly, the welfare of young people. (Smith, 2002a)

This book argues that these 'defining features' and 'key dimensions' constitute the defining characteristics of youth work because they give expression to a sense of *purpose* for youth work based on supporting young people's:

- Personal development: not merely in terms of the development of the individual but in terms of the *development of the person* – their sense of self, identity and the values that underpin their actions in the world.
- Social development: not in terms of 'life skills' or learning about social issues, but rather as the development of young people as *social beings in a social world*.

In so doing, youth work supports young people to learn from their experience; and develop the motivation and capacity to:

- Examine their values.
- Deliberate on the principles of their own moral judgements.
- Develop the skills and dispositions to make informed decisions that can be sustained through committed action.

Integral to this process is the issue of identity in terms of:

- Self-image: a person's description of self.
- Self-esteem: a person's evaluation of self, a crucial dimension of which is a person's adherence to moral and ethical standards. (Coleman and Hendry, 1999)

Philosophy

This makes youth work an exercise in moral philosophy insofar as it enables and supports young people to examine what they consider to be 'good or bad', 'right or wrong', 'desirable or undesirable' in relation to self and others – 'What sort of person am I?' 'What kind of relationships do I want?' 'What kind of community/society do I want to live in?' Fundamentally, youth work confronts Socrates' question, 'How should one live?' which is both singular and plural in the sense that it asks, 'How should I live?' as well as, 'How should anyone live?' (Williams, 1993).

Such an activity demands young people's voluntary participation since moral philosophising cannot be absent minded or mechanistic, and neither can it be hidden or coerced. Participation in moral philosophising requires that:

- Youth work's *purpose* as well as its processes is made explicit to young people.
- Young people engage in discussions that help them to clarify their understanding of what is involved.
- Young people give their conscious and informed consent to engage – not in the rock climbing, arts workshop, health discussion group or camping trip – but in the process of self-examination through which they increasingly integrate their values, actions and identity. (Young, 1999)

Participation in youth work is therefore more than simply taking part or having a say. Participation involves a process of conscious, critical self-reflection that can only be entered into voluntarily.

This participation becomes empowering as the young person increases their capacity to function well 'as a person, not as an instrument' (Fromm, 1993: 117). That is, as a person capable of autonomous rational judgement; acting from free will, voluntarily as opposed to acting 'under compulsion or from ignorance' (Aristotle, 1987: 66); a person who demonstrates:

- A disposition towards increasingly questioning taken-for-granted attitudes, assumptions and beliefs.
- An increasing integration of the values and purposes that permeate their actions and relationships.
- A sense of their own value and identity through different circumstances and pressures. (Pring, 1984)

For empowerment lies not only in the establishment of power-sharing structures or processes but importantly in the reclaiming of oneself as fully intelligent, fully powerful and fully human.

Such deliberations cannot, of course, take place in isolation since learning to become a certain kind of person is a function of the relationships within which we move, and which provide the context for whatever moral reflection we engage in (Kleinig, 1982). For as Aristotle observed, 'the fundamental moral and intellectual activities that go to make up a flourishing life cannot be continuously engaged in with pleasure and interest unless they are engaged in as part of shared activities with others who are themselves morally good persons' (cited in Cooper, 1980: 331). Youth work as an activity in moral philosophising is, therefore, necessarily based on conversation, association and integrity.

Also, in focusing on that particular moment typically known as adolescence, youth work engages with young people as they begin to explore the 'boundaries of freedom', examine how they see themselves and are seen by others, and reflect on their sense of 'personal identity' (Leighton, 1972). Youth work is, therefore, an age specific activity that focuses on young people not because they are disaffected or disengaged; not because they cause problems or have problems; but because they are in the process of creating themselves and developing the knowledge, skills and dispositions needed for lifelong reflection, learning and growth.

This is not to suggest that all young people are the same since they are, after-all, unique individuals who:

- Live in different circumstances e.g. in relation to housing, personal and familial relationships, urban/rural settings.

- Face different issues e.g. in terms of health, crime, employment.
- Have different interests e.g. sport, music, the environment.
- Aspire to different achievements e.g. in relation to educational achievement, career choices or life goals.

Young people are also different because some of them are women and others are men. Some are Black people, others white people. Some have a disability. Some identify as lesbian or gay. And they come from a range of class backgrounds and religious commitments.

However, in focusing on them as *young* people youth work respects and works with peer networks in ways that recognise:

- The similarities in young people's experiences because they are *young*; and
- The differences in young people's experiences as unique individuals who are also members of particular social groups.

Practice

All of this, however, brings us back to the beginning in the sense that, by its nature, youth work is based on a voluntary *relationship* with young people involving honesty, trust, respect and reciprocity; and a youth work *process* that enables and supports young people to learn from their experience and develop themselves as authentic human beings – i.e. people who know themselves and are true to themselves.

The youth work relationship is one in which the young person is accepted and valued; the youth worker has faith in the young person; shows concern and empathy; and takes account of their experiences, opinions and ideas. It is the kind of relationship described by the McNair Committee, as long ago as 1944, (HMSO, 1944: 103) as being 'a guide, philosopher and friend' to young people, which I previously elaborated as providing:

A steer for young people through the philosophical enquiry into the nature, significance and inter-relationship of their values and beliefs, based on a relationship of true friendship – [following Aristotle's definition of] – wanting for someone what one thinks good for his/her sake and not for one's own.

(Young, 1999: 82)

The youth work *process* is, therefore, a reflective exercise that enables and supports young people to:

- Learn from their experience.
- Develop their capacity to think critically.
- Engage in 'sense-making' as a process of continuous self-discovery and re-creation.

Art

The art of youth work is the ability to make and sustain such relationships with young people. In so doing, youth workers need to themselves develop the knowledge, skills and dispositions to engage with young people in the process of moral philosophising. The training and development of youth workers therefore needs to provide them with opportunities for their own self-exploration, examination of their own values, development of their own critical skills and enlargement of their own capacity for moral philosophy.

For in the end, adapting Louden's observation about teachers (quoted in Cortazzi, 1993), youth workers do not merely deliver youth work, they define it, interpret it and develop it. It is what youth workers think, what youth workers believe and what youth workers do in practice that ultimately shapes the kind of experience and learning that young people get.

The future for youth work

But none of this happens in a vacuum. Social policies and priorities change. Organisational structures are created and transmuted. Provision and practice are transformed. The question is, where is the future balance to lie between the following?:

- A concern for the welfare of young people as *people*; and a concern for the welfare of young people as *workers and citizens*.
- The provision of things to do and places to go; and the provision of opportunities for young people's personal and social development.
- A focus on informal education; and a focus on prevention and effective early intervention.
- An approach that treats young people as 'customers' who help to shape the services they receive; and an approach that treats young people as 'partners' in the process of learning and development.
- A perception of young people as young people; and a perception of young people as alienated, anti-social, drug and alcohol abusing delinquents in need of social integration.
- A view of young people as achievers of outcomes; and a view of young people as creators of their own lives and the communities of which they are a part.

The hope is that this book will act as a reminder of what youth work was, is and ought to be, and in so doing will help to:

- Support the continuing contribution of youth work as a distinct practice in work with young people;

- Clarify the differences between youth work and other forms of work with young people so as to inform the appropriate contribution of youth work to the ever changing arrangements for services to young people;
- Illuminate the ways in which youth worker training and development could be built on in order to enable practitioners to develop the knowledge, skills and dispositions necessary to successfully undertake youth work as an exercise in moral philosophy.

Finally, I make no apology for the quotations from youth workers and young people included here, for whilst social policies and organisational structures change, the philosophy of youth work does not. So as dated as these quotations are, they nonetheless continue to exemplify the core purpose and principles of youth work, and the practice that is in danger of being left behind.

Chapter 2

Philosophy

In one of Plato's dialogues Socrates asks Laches the question 'what is courage?' Laches' response is immediate – a man who does not run away in battle. However, as Socrates demonstrates, Laches' answer is not a definition of courage, but rather one particular example of it. Socrates then asks 'What is that common quality, which is the same in all cases, and which is called courage?' (Plato trans., 1970: 117). In other words, 'what is the *nature* of courage?'

This book asks that same question of youth work. 'What is that common quality, which is the same in all cases, and which is called youth work?' In other words, what is the *nature* of youth work? This represents an examination of the philosophy of youth work since philosophy is concerned with the *nature* of things. For while we are continually offered examples of youth work in terms of the issues to be addressed (crime, sex, health, drugs, education/employment/training), the methods used (detached work, group-work, peer education), activities undertaken (outdoor pursuits, arts, sport), roles of the youth worker (befriender, advocate, mentor), it is rarely the case that we consider the *common qualities* that enable all such examples to be known collectively as 'youth work'. That is, as a distinct activity in its own right; and one able to be distinguished from other forms of work with young people.

Of course, youth work literature is littered with references to informal education, and young people's personal and social education. But what does this mean? Particularly when a whole range of professionals within the education, training and employment field, youth justice, formal education, health and social welfare all now lay claim to some form of informal education that supports young people's personal development and informed decision making.

Even youth work's commitment to the principles of education, participation, empowerment and equality of opportunity is insufficient to confirm its 'uniqueness' since youth work does not own the monopoly on such principles. Indeed, ideas about participation, empowerment, equality, diversity and community cohesion punctuate almost every aspect of 21st century social policy.

In addition, describing youth work in terms of issues, methods and activities reveals little about what it is (its nature) or the reason for which it is done (its purpose). This is crucial since the assertion here is that youth work's particular contribution to young people's lives cannot be understood by reference to 'reach' or target groups. Youth work's uniqueness can only be demonstrated through an understanding of its fundamental *nature* and *purpose*.

Emerging purpose

Concern about the development of young people's values and the 'sort of people' they are and are to become is, and always has been, a fundamental feature of youth work thinking and practice. However, while early pioneers were often likely to conceive this in terms of the inculcation of particular values, an examination of youth service reports and commentaries reveals changing interpretations, which focus increasingly on the importance of young people questioning ideas, attitudes and values.

For example, at its establishment in 1844, the YMCA adopted the following statement:

> *The Young Men's Christian Association seeks to unite those young men who, regarding Jesus Christ as their God and Saviour, according to the Holy Scriptures, desire to be His disciples in their faith and in their life, and to associate their efforts for the extension of His Kingdom amongst young men.*

(Reproduced in YMCA, 1987)

Similarly, the Object of the Boys' Brigade, established in 1883, is stated as 'The advancement of Christ Kingdom amongst boys and the promotion of habits of obedience, reverence, discipline, self-respect and all that tends towards true Christian manliness.' Davies (1999a) also noted that the Boys' Brigade specifically required its officers to 'promote cleanliness, discipline and obedience', and 'encourage physical, mental and moral culture' (Davies, 1999a: 9).

So while much of early youth work (particularly with boys) was framed in religious, and often militaristic, terms it nonetheless made clear the 'sort of people' it hoped would develop. That is, people who exhibited the qualities of obedience, discipline, punctuality, cleanliness, reverence, and self-respect; people who participated in public service and had a clear religious commitment (Davies and Gibson, 1967; Milson, 1970; Eggleston, 1976; Booton, 1985; Smith, 1988; Davies, 1999a).

This clarity persists within many of the traditional voluntary youth organisations, for example, within the Scout/Guide Law, which explicitly identifies the 'sort of person' a Scout or Guide is meant to be.

The Guide Law:
A guide is honest, reliable and can be trusted.
A guide is helpful and uses time and abilities wisely.
A guide faces challenge and learns from her experiences.
A guide is a good friend and a sister to all guides.
A guide is polite and considerate.
A guide respects all living things and takes care of the world around her.

Indeed, Lord Baden-Powell believed that the aim of scouting was to set young people on the right road to citizenship through discipline, self-reliance, self-sacrifice and patriotism (cited in Davies and Gibson, 1967: 41).

However, alongside this Booton also observed the existence of the 'self-conscious, systematic practice of youth work', which according to him, began with the establishment of clubs for girls in the 1860s in which:

> ... *women youth workers refer to a multiplicity of clubs and agencies which are sufficiently similar for them to identify at a level of common understanding. To contrast these with an early account of boys' clubs work such as Pilkingston's* [contained in the same Volume] *is to demonstrate immediately the sense of a considered practice as distinguished from mere undifferentiated work.*

(Booton, 1985: 39)

This observation led Booton to assert that:

> *In general it is true to say that work with girls* [1860–1890] *was philosophically determined in conceptual terms that emphasised such things as relationships, welfare-support and frequently, a 'political' dimension to individual and collective awareness, whilst that with boys often remained at a level of amusement, 'discipline', 'training' and 'character'.*

(Booton, 1985: 21)

Therefore, as Smith (1988), Davies (1999a) and others have observed, the origins of youth work lie in a combination of the work of voluntary (often specifically religious) organisations and philanthropic benefactors whose main purpose was to provide a charitable means of association and physical activity; and to socialise young people into the prevailing social mores and political values. At the same time, there were *others* who acknowledged and addressed the damaging consequences of the prevailing social conditions, for example, the 'damaging consequences for young women of the monotony of the workshop life' (Davies, 1999a: 8). Indeed, Carpenter and Young (1986) noted that it was from a Working Girls' Club that the demand came for legislation regarding the working conditions of underground workrooms.

Yet despite these 'oppositional' stances, there remained a broad level of consistency regarding common purpose – in the sense that most of the early voluntary youth organisations' sense of purpose reflected some balance between compassionate benevolence and anxiety to maintain the given social order. Davies' (1999a) summary of the main conclusions of other key commentators therefore suggested that early youth work exhibited a mixed set of motives which included:

- A sense of compassion to help those 'less fortunate'.
- Anxieties about the 'social and moral unreliability of youth'.
- A determination to 'win and hold these young people to a religious faith'.
- A determination to 'moralise young people – to instil in them some bedrock social attitudes and habits'.
- A political agenda 'focused increasingly on thwarting the class conflicts which were re-emerging both within and outside parliament and the threat that these posed to what was still largely seen as a given social order.' (Davies, 1999a: 8–10)

Co-ordinated provision

However, the impact of the First World War (with the recruitment of young men into the armed forces and tensions and problems at home, including increasing juvenile crime) was to give rise to a hugely significant shift towards co-ordinating the efforts of the disparate voluntary organisations.

A Home Office committee chaired by Charles Russell recommended that juvenile organisation committees should be set up locally to 'coordinate and stimulate youth provision' (Davies, 1999a: 15). In addition, the establishment of a national Juvenile Organisation Committee (chaired by Russell) brought, for the first time, 'voluntary youth organisations into a policy-making relationship with the state' (Davies, 1999a: 15). These wartime powers were formalised by the 1918 and 1921 Education Acts, which empowered local authorities to make grants to clubs and youth groups, and sanctioned them to set up their own juvenile organisation committees where voluntary organisations had failed to do so previously.

Yet, while the post 1900s witnessed an increase in youth provision and the founding of many of the foremost voluntary youth organisations (e.g. Boy Scout Association, 1907, Girl Guide Association, 1910, National Association of Girls' Clubs,1911, National Association of Boys' Clubs, 1925), the second major push towards a co-ordinated 'service for youth' was to come as a result of concerns about the physical health of the nation and especially about whether young men were fit enough to fight for their country in what many perceived as an inevitable second war in Europe.

In 1937 the Physical Training and Recreation Act empowered local authorities to pay for facilities designed to raise the level of national fitness and on 27th November 1939 the Board of Education published Circular 1486, *The Service of Youth*. With this circular, the government took upon itself a 'direct responsibility for youth welfare'. In so doing, it introduced the institutional arrangement known as the youth service, and described youth work as the 'social and physical development of boys and girls' and the development of their 'body, mind and spirit' (Board of Education, 1939).

A year later, following the outbreak of the Second World War, the Board of Education referred to the need 'to develop the whole personality of individual boys and girls to enable them to take their place as full members of a free community' (Board of Education, 1940).

Whilst less tangible than earlier formulations, these definitions nonetheless contained implicit beliefs about the 'sort of people' or 'personalities' that youth work should seek to 'produce', so that in 1945, the Youth Advisory Council stated that 'whatever the activity, and whatever the precise motif, the lessons to be learned are the same, co-operation, tolerance, free decision and joint responsibility' (Ministry of Education, 1945), thereby clearly identifying the values and qualities to be encouraged in young people.

Educational purposes

In urging all local education authorities to establish youth committees and to seek the co-operation of voluntary organisations in providing a comprehensive service for young people between the ages of 14 and 20, the government indicated that youth work was both an education service and a service for which it wished to take some responsibility.

This commitment was confirmed in Sections 41(b) and 53(1) and (2) of the Education Act 1944 which placed a duty on all local education authorities to ensure that the facilities for further education provided in their area included adequate facilities for recreation, social and physical training, co-operating as appropriate with 'any voluntary societies or bodies whose objects include provision of facilities or the organisation of activities of a similar character'. This, as amended by Section 120 of the 1988 Education Reform Act, provided the legislative base for youth service provision by local education authorities.

Between 1939 and 1982, successive government circulars and commissioned reports all contributed to illuminating, re-interpreting and re-shaping the purpose of youth work. Therefore, the significance of Circular 1486 was not merely that it established the youth service as a distinct service and part of the state maintained education service, but importantly, that it consolidated existing provision and practice by identifying the purpose of the proposed 'comprehensive service' as providing for the 'social and physical development of boys and girls between the ages of 14 and 20 who have ceased full-time education.' The object of which was to help young people develop their 'body, mind and spirit' (Board of Education, 1939).

At the end of the war, in 1945, the National Youth Advisory Council's report *The Purpose and the Content of the Youth Service* expressed the purpose of the youth service as to promote and provide opportunities for participating in activities which:

- are carried out in a community different in its nature from school or work;
- are voluntarily undertaken;
- are complementary to other activities; and
- are approached from the standpoint of recreation. (Ministry of Education, 1945: 7)

These ideas about the purpose of youth work were to become refined in the statement by Sir John Redcliffe Maud (then Permanent Secretary at the Ministry of Education) who stated that the aim of the youth service was:

> . . . to offer individual young people in their leisure time, opportunities of various kinds, complementary to those at home, formal education and work, to discover and develop their personal resources of body, mind and spirit and thus better equip themselves to live the life of mature, creative and responsible members of a free society.
>
> (King George's Jubilee Trust, 1951: 13)

Personal, social and political education

From this point onwards the exercise of defining purpose in youth work became, practically, an exercise in re-interpreting Maud's earlier statement in the light of contemporary society. For example, the Albemarle Report (HMSO, 1960) commented that:

> We believe this [Maud's] statement should, to gain its full force, be seen against the contemporary background we have described – of a society at once so complex, so formal and so fluid that its conflicting pressures can substantially discourage good development. The aim of the youth service is not to remove tensions so as to reach towards some hypothetical condition of 'adjustment' to individual or social life. It is to help towards ensuring that those tensions which are social accidents, often both fruitless and oppressive, shall not submerge the better possibilities of children during their adolescence.
>
> (HMSO, 1960: para 135)

The Report also expanded on Maud's notion of 'leisure time' opportunities by introducing, into the youth work vocabulary, the terms 'social and informal education':

The youth service is an integral part of the education system, since it provides for the continued social and informal education of young people in terms most likely to bring them to maturity, those of responsible personal choice.

(HMSO, 1960: para 351)

The Albemarle Report reaffirmed the importance of 'a sense of fellowship', 'mutual respect and tolerance' (HMSO, 1960: para 135), 'responsible personal choice' (para 351) and 'the capacity for making sound judgements' (para 136).

Therefore, whilst the Report focused on young people's *personal development* (e.g. in encouraging a 'sense of achievement', and personal qualities such as the capacity to make 'sound judgements') – it also affirmed the importance of their *social education* (e.g. in encouraging a sense of fellowship, and personal qualities such as 'mutual respect and tolerance'). And in this regard, the Report specifically addressed the need for young people to question accepted ideas, attitudes and standards in society:

The youth service should not be seen to offer something packaged – a 'way of life', a 'set of values', 'a code' as though these were things which came ready-made, upon the asking, without being tested in living experience . . . If they feel the need, young people must have the liberty to question cherished ideas, attitudes and standards and if necessary to reject them.

(HMSO, 1960: para 141: 142)

Nine years later a further report, *Youth and Community Work in the 70s* remarked that Maud's definition had not 'spent its force' but needed to be given 'fresh interpretations and emphases in the light of contemporary society' (HMSO, 1969: para 152). As such, the Report re-affirmed the relationship between youth work and social education and stated that:

The primary goal of youth work is the social education of young people. Such a definition is not unimportant since, as we have seen the aim changes as society changes. We are not so much concerned today as in the past with basic education, or with economic needs, or with the communication of an agreed belief or value system; but we are concerned to help young people to create their place in a changing society and it is their critical involvement in their community which is the goal.

(HMSO, 1969: para 152)

The concept of 'critical involvement' included:

- Young people's active participation in the learning process through exercising 'choice in the form and content of what is learnt'.
- The self-government of provision.
- The establishment of youth councils.
- Young people's active participation in a 'participant democracy' and contribution to the formation of ideas and public opinion. (HMSO, 1969)

These ideas of participation introduced *political education* onto the youth work agenda insofar as:

> *Politics is concerned with life and how people live together. We see the new service providing many opportunities for young people to discuss matters of controversy and to share in the formation of public opinion.*
>
> (HMSO, 1969: para 211)

The report of the Thompson Committee, *Experience and Participation* (HMSO, 1982) proclaimed 'virtual unanimity' amongst those consulted by the Review Group that:

> *The fundamental purpose of the youth service is to provide programmes of personal development comprising in shorthand terms, social and political education. The twin aims of this purpose are thus affirmation and involvement – affirming an individual in his or her proper identity and involving an individual in relationships with other individuals and institutions.*
>
> (HMSO, 1982: para 7.3)

Experience and Participation also commented on the Maud formulation observing that 'this definition which comprehensively recapitulated pre-war and wartime experience has insights which are of enduring value today, but it ignored too much' (HMSO, 1982: para 1.7) namely, the social, economic and political contexts in which young people live their lives; and the powerful impact of these on their personal development. *Experience and Participation* specifically referred to the damaging effects of racism, sexism and attitudes towards disabled people. (HMSO, 1982)

For example:

> *Racism damages those who practise it as well as those who suffer from it. It is a deep tragedy for British society that the cultural diversity which should be a source of enjoyment and enrichment is liable to give rise to expressions of violence, harassment and antipathy which impoverish and threaten the lives of many and especially young people.*
>
> (HMSO, 1982: para 2.7)

Elsewhere in the Report the Thompson Committee remarked that the youth service 'uncritically mirrors sexist attitudes in society' which 'it has carried into elements of its practice and philosophy' and suggested:

> *Ingrained attitudes can be challenged and unconscious assumptions brought to the surface. In short, the youth service curriculum should be committed to the eradication of sexist attitudes.*
>
> (HMSO, 1982: para 6.54)

Following the publication of the Thompson Report many local youth services conducted reviews that resulted in policy changes and the formulation of new statements of purpose. Doug Smith's observation was that while the primary aims of many youth services were often conceived in 'individual' terms, alongside this were two further strands of emerging youth service aims:

> *First, and this has been developing over a number of years, is an increasing recognition by the Service of the social and political context within which young people live. This recognition generally takes the form of explicitly acknowledging some of the major structural divisions in British society, especially those of class, gender and race, which help determine young people's views and concerns and which materially affect their social and political circumstances.*
>
> (Smith, D. 1987: 19)

The second strand focused on the role of the service as an advocate with and for young people – 'the movement towards recognising young people's interests and viewing the work of the Service in relation to young people in a collective sense' (Smith, D. 1987: 20).

Education, participation, empowerment and equality of opportunity

In July 1989 the Department of Education and Science announced a series of three national conferences for the youth service. This initiative signalled a change in emphasis from government support for deliberative work by committees to 'conferences with senior practitioners designed to lead to concrete action and the implementation of agreed change by those in both local authority and voluntary sectors of the service' (DES Press Release, 14 July 1989).

The first conference, entitled 'Towards a Core Curriculum for the Youth Service', was held in December 1989. Its central task was 'to reach a clearer understanding about the role of the youth service within education provision and of the curriculum necessary to fulfil this role' (NYB, 1990: 65). The conference, attended by over 220 delegates from voluntary organisations and local authority youth services, confirmed that the youth service was education focused. However, conference participants believed that extensive consultations were needed in order to ascertain whether or not a 'nationally agreed core curriculum' could be determined.

After a series of wide ranging consultations within both voluntary organisations and local authority services, the Second Ministerial Conference for the Youth Service (November 1990) recommended that:

The purpose of youth work is to redress all forms of inequality and to ensure equality of opportunity for all young people to fulfil their potential as empowered individuals and members of groups and communities and to support young people during the transition to adulthood.

(Statement of Purpose NYB, 1991: 16)

The conference report also stated that youth work offers young people opportunities that are:

Educative – *enabling young people to gain the skills, knowledge and attitudes needed to identify, advocate and pursue their rights and responsibilities as individuals and as members of groups and communities locally, nationally and internationally;*

Designed to promote equality of opportunity
- Through the challenging of oppressions such as racism and sexism and all those which spring from differences of culture, race, language, sexual identity, gender, disability, age, religion and class; and
- Through the celebration of the diversity and strengths which arise from those differences.

Participative *through a voluntary relationship with young people in which young people are partners in the learning process and decision making structures which affect their own and other young people's lives and their environment.*

Empowering *supporting young people to understand and act on the personal, social and political issues which affect their lives, the lives of others and the communities of which they are a part.*

(NYB, 1991: 16)

The third conference (1992) focused on planning and evaluation.

However, the original intention that the Ministerial Conferences should result in a nationally agreed statement of purpose and a 'core curriculum' for the youth service (including common learning outcomes, methods for identifying learning outcomes, and performance indicators) did not come to pass, and the initiative ended, as Bernard Davies put it, not with a bang but with a 'ministerial whimper' (1999b: 136).

But the youth service's failure to agree a 'core curriculum' did not eradicate the need for a clear statement of what constituted its core purpose or purposes. Indeed in 1998, Tom Wylie (Chief Executive of the National Youth Agency) suggested that:

What would most help the youth service nationwide is a clearly expressed focus in respect of its core purposes, its primary target groups and the distinctive programmes and services which it should be offering.

(Wylie, 1998: 25)

Various definitions followed. For example, in 1999 Becsky and Perrett described youth work as follows:

Youth work supports young people in their transition from childhood to responsible adulthood, encourages their social development and individual fulfilment, and helps them to engage fully in society. It is concerned primarily with young people's personal and social development and is critically informed by a set of beliefs which include a commitment to equal opportunity, and to young people as partners in learning and in decision making. Youth work offers educational programmes and projects that complement and support learning in school and college in which young people choose to be involved. It offers a constructive and educational use of leisure time. It helps young people to achieve and fulfil their potential and to make choices about their lives by offering them information, advice and support.

(Becsky and Perrett, 1999: 52)

The National Occupational Standards for Youth Work in the UK (January 2002) identified the purpose of youth work as:

To work with young people to facilitate their personal, social and educational development, and enable them to gain a voice, influence and place in society in a period of their transitions from dependence to independence . . . Informed by Youth Work values, the role of the youth worker is therefore to work with young people in ways that are:

- *Educative;*
- *Participative;*
- *Empowering; and*
- *Promote equality of opportunity and social inclusion.*

(Paulo NTO, 2002)

The National Youth Agency Guide to Youth Work and Youth Service stated:

Youth work helps young people learn about themselves, others and society, through informal educational activities which combine enjoyment, chal-lenge and learning. Youth workers work primarily with young people aged between 13 and 19, but may in some cases extend this to those aged 11 to 13 and 19 to 25. Their work seeks to promote young people's personal and social development and enable them to have a voice, influence and place in their communities and society as a whole.

(NYA, 2003: 4)

Consistency and continuity

Throughout these developments there has been a consistent theme, which persisted from the late Victorian period through to the 1990s, a theme that revealed the *nature* of youth work as essentially concerned with young people's values and the development of moral and ethical standards – from obedience and tolerance to challenging oppression and celebrating diversity.

Also, despite the changing emphasis over the years, much of the underpinning ideas about the nature and purpose of youth work could still be found in the practice of those interviewed in connection with this work in the late 1990s. For example, in terms of the commitment to young people's emotional, mental, physical and spiritual growth as identified by Sir John Redcliffe Maud (King George's Jubilee Trust 1951: 13):

We have the stated aims about emotional, mental, physical and spiritual growth. So we're not specifically interested in someone's academic ability. In terms of the physical some people would say that we don't do that very well whereas others see camping as a physical activity. Certainly, we're not as sporty as we used to be and there are a lot of people who regret that. So right now there's a move to think some more about sport but not competitive sport necessarily – things like girls' football where they're developing the skills with a ball rather than having to get into a league. What we're trying to do is give a balance so you get your outdoors and your arts in Guiding. You don't have to choose between one or the other.

In terms of the emotional, some of that's about being with other people and being in control of thinking about the effect on others of what you've said or done. Learning about relationships. There are a lot of Ranger Units now that are getting into things like sessions with Relate focused on taking control of a relationship, deciding what you're looking for in a relationship, not being put upon and issues like that. I think that's probably a response to the teenage pregnancy issue.

The spiritual dimension is quite difficult in Guiding because for some people this is very much linked to the church. And in fact some units are clearly linked to a church or, for reasons of cost, use church premises. But spirituality is not just about religion. It's something to do with a connection with nature – going to the mountains and feeling a part of the world. Sleeping under the stars. Just being in the environment and remembering that you are only human. It can be really simple. For example, we had a young woman with a disability in our unit and then one day we were all sitting on the grass and we realised that she'd never sat on the grass. She wanted to join us so we helped her out of her wheelchair and she was completely stunned. She just couldn't believe it.

Interviewees also cited examples of practice that reflect the attention to 'responsible personal choice' and 'sense of achievement' to which the Albemarle Report (HMSO, 1960) referred:

I'm into creating opportunities for young people to succeed, experience a sense of achievement and grow in self-esteem. That's how I see youth work. Increasing young people's expectations of life and raising their horizons.

We have a vested interest in developing young people who are able to reflect on their experience, consider different courses of action and the effect on other people, make choices, who have the confidence to bring about change or influence their lives and who hopefully will not do that at the expense of other people but with other people.

The notion of self-government, a sense of community and young people's understanding of their 'place in a changing society' as underlined in *Youth and Community Work in the 70s* (HMSO, 1969) can also be seen in contemporary practice:

Self government ranges from being able to choose what your Guide unit is going to do – probably from a prescribed list – say choose four activities from a list of eight or something like that; through to a Ranger unit that sets its own constitution and programmes and works it out for itself – writes its own letters, booking speakers and venues, organising the mini-bus, sorting out the catering arrangements. Just doing everything.

Youth work is about enabling young people to find themselves. It's about them being able to look at where they're at in their lives, the way they interact with other people and feeling that they can make an impact on others around them. Maybe this is really simplistic but I feel if I can make an impact on, say, three young people during their lifetime which means that they take on some of the values about how people treat each other and offer that to the people they come into contact with then you'd have a kind of domino effect. And that could actually create a sense of community, a connection, a sense of being a human being that is far bigger than just you or me.

What I've always tried to do in my work with young people is to help them explore where they are at in their life, their relationships and how they see themselves within society – their position, their schooling, what they do when they come along to the club, how they interact with each other, what their demands are, what their requests are, how they feel, how they want to be treated as young people. But in order to work effectively with young people with disabilities you also have to take into consideration a lot of the external influences. More so, I think, than in mainstream youth work. So I have to think about parental wishes and influences. Particularly when you are talking about personal relationships, sexual relationships and what that actually means, but this is not to say the young people's wishes are ignored.

Similarly, the Thompson Report (HMSO, 1982) emphasised the need for young people to have the experience of being valued, and opportunities to understand their 'identity'. And again this is reflected in the practice of interviewees:

> Youth work is about enabling young people to think about themselves and their life. Who they are as human beings and what their contribution is and can be to society. It's about giving them positive strokes and letting them know that they exist and are valuable human beings. That's regardless of what they've experienced and where they've come from. It's just seeing them as they come through the door, respecting them and not judging them.

Finally, interviewees' practice also reflects the Second Ministerial Conference's (NYA, 1991) commitment to education, participation, empowerment and equality of opportunity:

> Youth work is about empowerment – supporting young people to increase their confidence in expressing themselves, their needs, their desires, their fulfilments. It's about them being able to communicate with other people and make constructive decisions while taking into account the different options available and the possible consequences.

> Education, capacity building, empowerment and equality of opportunity are all part of a community development approach that starts where young people are at, is dictated by their needs, goes at their pace, and is flexible to fit different situations. Even though this may look casual to the outsider, or even the young people, it represents very deliberate interventions by the youth worker.

Young people's views

Yet, despite the apparently nebulous nature of youth work young people themselves are often very clear about its nature and purpose:

> Youth work isn't a job. You can't look at it like it's just a job unless you are in it for the wrong reasons. Like if you were just out to get a job and you go into youth work you won't really enjoy it. To be a youth worker you have to want to encourage young people's development – no matter who they are. They help your development socially and with your confidence. They encourage you to do activities, go out and meet people. You start doing things that you don't normally do. They make you talk and you can talk about anything really. They're there to have fun with you and look out for you and at the same time help you to discover all the aspects of life that you may not discover by yourself. Like before I got into youth work I just stayed in at weekends. I didn't do anything. But now we go out, sometimes we do fund raising events and all sorts of things. I would never

have dreamed of doing some of the stuff we've done like face painting and handing out flyers because I was really self-conscious. But I did it and it was a big thing for me. We also did a parachute jump, which was quite good. The group I'm in now we just think of as many bizarre things as we can and just do them because we're never going to get a chance again.

The role of the youth worker is to help young people build their confidence and realise that they are needed and valued and that they can do loads of super things – helping them to respect others and have a community feeling. It's about making them feel like they may be different but there's still a right track that you should be on as a person. So the youth worker helps you to find that right track because they see what you are capable of. But you choose that track as a young person because they can't force you to do anything. If I'd never met . . . [the worker] I wouldn't be so headstrong about the right thing. I would have been headstrong about the wrong thing. But now I see the importance of things like the work ethic, respecting others, appreciating your culture and just not being nasty and realising that the world doesn't revolve around you.

I've learnt about what sort of person I am through meeting different people everyday. I think you also learn about what sort of person you want to be when you are older. Like role models in a sense that help you to become more self aware about who you are and where you fit into all of this. And then you start thinking. Because when you're at school you're just confined to school. Come home, do your homework, have an argument with your parents. Next morning you get up, have your breakfast and go to school again. But being with youth workers it's completely different. Since I've known them I've become less negative. I feel like I have something to offer now.

I've developed an awful lot as a person in the four years that I've been coming here. I think if I hadn't have come here I would never have learnt what I've learnt about how to treat people in a better way and how people react to different situations. I've become more considerate and more caring and I understand a lot more about different people and their different backgrounds and experiences. I've also learnt that there is a lot more I could do because although I have some good qualities, like being reliable and trustworthy, there are also some bad qualities that I have. In time I need to develop those bad aspects and improve on the good ones. What I'd really like is to be able to say, 'What you see is what you get'. No false pretences about what I believe. No fake outside image. Just trying to be down to earth and natural. That's how I'd like people to see me.

What is remarkable about these quotations is not the differences in expression or language regarding the nature and purpose of youth work, but rather, the consistency in meaning and inference that emerges from both youth workers and young people. This is particularly striking in terms of their expressed commitment to enabling and supporting young people's capacity to:

- 'Grow' as human beings;
- Take charge of themselves and their lives; and
- Participate in decision-making processes and 'political' activity in their community and society at large.

Over the last ten years most of my work has been a process of getting young people to explore alternative beliefs and value systems. When you are young you almost believe that this is how life will always be for you. So in claiming the values of your peers or school or capitalism you've not necessarily had the space to explore what you really believe. That opportunity has not been provided in schools because over the past ten years they have become very task and exam focused which means that the possibility of exploring what's not actually on the curriculum is no longer there in any real sense. There is personal and social education, which does provide young people with some information – for example about drugs or contraception or HIV or whatever. But what it tends not to do is get young people to engage on a deeper level about how they actually think, feel and act given all of this information.

My mission isn't to make young people be something. My mission is to explore with young people their potential and the wealth of life options available to them. When you are young you don't necessarily feel you have any options apart from keeping up with your peer group. For instance, you may feel that you have to do something against your own values in order to get those trainers or engage in sexual practices before you were ready because there were pressures upon you. But if you've given young people a chance to consider not only their options but, the possibility of choice, then it becomes clear that there is a range of value systems and you can choose any of them.

Youth work is about engaging with young people on an agenda that is about knowledge of the self and how young people perceive the world and their place within that world. So if we were organising a dance workshop we would ensure that the tutor we engage is aware of our agenda. Yes, they may be doing street dancing, hip hop or whatever but what we want conveyed to young people is an understanding of the link that that style of dance has with the long tradition of Black dance whether that's from West Africa or the Harlem Renaissance. The important thing is to understand the continuity. Not that nothing is new but understanding that what they come with is a transformation of what already is. And that they are connected to a long line of people who have enabled them to exist in the way that they exist here today.

The common quality reflected in all of these expressions of the work can be seen, therefore, as a concern not with the methods of youth work nor the issues or activities in which young people engage, but rather, a central concern for young people's development as *people*. That is:

- Their sense of themselves as human beings and members of particular social groups (**identity**); and
- Their developing values and value system (**ethical standards**).

'Adolescence' and 'youth'

Since the youth service specifically works with young people in the age range 11–25, albeit with a priority on 13 to 19 year olds, before addressing the issues of identity and ethical standards it is necessary to examine 'adolescence', 'adulthood' and 'youth' as central concepts for youth work.

Adolescence

The concept of 'adolescence' is central to the concept of 'youth work'. Not simply because youth work focuses its attention on a particular age range but also because 'adolescence' is typically portrayed as involving various transitions, for example in relation to clarity about rights, roles and responsibilities (Coleman, Catan and Dennison, 1997). Specifically within youth work, 'adolescence' is often perceived as a period of transition 'to adulthood' or alternatively, the transition from 'dependence to independence or interdependence'.

> When I think about it, I think the 'transition' idea is like going on a journey. When you go on a journey you need a guide especially if it's a journey that you've never been on before and young people haven't been on this journey before. Now that guide may be a book or some sort of information or sometimes it's a person. As I unravel this it seems to me that young people are on this journey where the difference is that the guide doesn't tell you what to do. The guide gives you information and sometimes advice. And you engage with the guide in a process that's about figuring out which way to go. Sometimes the road may take a turn you didn't expect and you may end up in a swamp. At which point the guide may have to rescue you and help you out – help you back onto your journey again. Actually, it's a journey that we all travel. But as we get older we gain more experience that hopefully we learn from. One of the things we learn is that life has a lot of swamps. The trick is to see them coming and learn how to avoid them.
>
> If young people are in transition then we have to be able to say when that journey ends. For me, being an adult means being able to make decisions and accept the consequences of those decisions. It is when you are clear about

what you are and are not prepared to do in terms of what is acceptable to you as a person. It's about having a solid set of principles that you use to measure your actions.

However, despite the emphasis on the 'personal journey', it is also accepted that 'adolescence' is a social phenomenon to be understood in relation to the social setting of the individual, the pressure of social expectations, and the relative influence of different agents of socialisation (Coleman, 1992). This is a social setting within which young people are 'neither a homogeneous group nor a static one' (Jones quoted in Wyn and White, 1997: 8).

Adulthood

If adolescence is a period of 'transition to adulthood' then we must be able to identify when that transition ends. That is, we need to be able to define the concept of 'adulthood'. Kiernan (cited in Morrow and Richards, 1996) defines adulthood as involving:

• Finishing full-time education;
• Entry into the labour market;
• Leaving home;
• The establishment of an independent household;
• Entry into marriage or cohabitation; and
• Parenthood.

In addition, Jones and Wallace (cited in Morrow and Richards, 1996) also include the acquisition of full citizenship.

Yet, as one interviewee commented:

It's very easy to say that young people with disabilities have the same rights as any other young person but in reality that is not the truth. There are all sorts of pressures from significant others and services available to young people and so on, and emotional pressures as well that act to create situations whereby young people are not supported or allowed to exercise the independence that is usually associated with adulthood. That anxiety and fear and desire to both control and protect starts almost from the day that young person is born and so often has very little to do with the actual abilities, capabilities or capacity of the young person concerned.

Morrow and Richards themselves classify 'the normative ideal of contemporary adult status' into four main categories political or legal adulthood, financial or economic adulthood, social and sexual adulthood, and parenthood (1996: 10). They also assert that major changes in each of these aspects of transition result in an overall disconnection and complex (rather than linear) series of 'transitions'.

Indeed, as Merton and Wylie point out:

Youth work has long seen itself as encouraging the personal development of young people during their years of transition from childhood to adulthood. The very notion of such transitions is now being challenged: certainly the transitions have become longer, more complex and much more risky. Young people have to negotiate individual paths through education and training and into the labour market. They have to work out how best to move from the home of their childhood to independent living, and to choose how they want to deal with personal relationships, their health and family life. Moreover, these processes no longer naturally take a linear form – into work, then independent housing, followed by family formation. They are combined in different ways and they can be reversed if young people experience difficulties in sustaining employment, living independently or maintaining relationships.

(2002: 1)

Interviewees were, however, not only aware of the complexities of young people's 'transition' but also challenged the very notion of young people's transitional status:

I don't think young people's transitional status is at all clear. It's not like leaving school at 16 and becoming an adult. Mass unemployment has completely changed that. Also, young people are developing their aware-ness of life at quite an early stage. They are very aware of sex and issues around sex. They are aware of a lot of things that I certainly wasn't aware of at their age. So I think the experience is just about moving on and learning and gaining experience. And I think that applies to adults as much as it does to young people because I don't see a clear demarcation between what young people know and their experience; and what older people know and their experience.

I think the idea that young people are in 'transition' is insulting. It gives the impression that young people are unfinished 'products' or 'work in progress' which can be shaped by whatever the adult population decides is 'in their best interest'. It does not confer the status of citizen on them which in turn does not see them as having a right to be involved in decision making.

As perceived by these workers, young people are not 'work in progress'. Their understanding is rather of an on-going experience within which young people's present (as opposed to future) lives should be seen as something of value, in itself. In addition, there is concern that young people's 'transitional status' may lead to others deciding what is 'in their best interest'. Intrinsic to that concern, is the desire for young people to be acknowledged as citizens and included in decision making.

However, while it may be difficult to distinguish a clear 'demarcation between what young people know and their experience; and what older people know and their experience' it is not suggested that the experience of being a young person is the same as that of being an adult. The point is that young people's knowledge and experience are not necessarily exclusive to them in the sense that what they may know about (e.g. sex) some adults may also know about; and what they may experience (e.g. unemployment) some adults may also experience. Nonetheless, the particular experience of being young is not a biological reality. As Wyn and White point out:

Age is a concept which is assumed to refer to a biological reality. However, the meaning and the experience of age, and of the process of ageing, is subject to historical and cultural processes ... whereby age is socially constructed, institutionalised and controlled in historically and culturally specific ways.

(Wyn and White, 1997: 9–11)

Therefore, it is not the objective reality of age that is contested but rather the subjective 'meaning' with which 'youth' has been imbued. In other words, whereas 'adolescence' has been conceptualised in terms of psychology, 'youth' has been constructed in sociological terms and thereby, embedded with particular 'meanings'.

Youth

Griffin (1993) identified a number of discourses that construct 'youth' broadly in two ways – either in terms of 'youth as trouble' and therefore in need of control, or 'youth in trouble' and therefore in need of protection. She also comments that:

In general, young men especially if they are working class and/or black are especially likely to be the focus of policies that operate with a 'youth as trouble' discourse. Young women, however, are more likely to be dealt with under the aegis of a 'youth in trouble' discourse.

(Griffin, 1997: 22)

Griffin goes on to make a number of other key observations:

- Dominant representations of youth are partly about setting young people apart from children and adults, as a transition point between two separate age stages.
- Such representations also make distinctions between different groups of young people (e.g. on the basis of gender, 'race', class, sexuality) in terms of discourses of deviance, disaffection and protection.

- Dominant representations of youth in social welfare policies (and main-stream academic literature) have targeted specific groups of young people as being in need of 'surveillance', 'protection' and/or 'care'. (1997: 24)

'Youth' and youth work

Youth work focuses on young people at that particular moment in their lives when they are developing their awareness, seeking answers and, crucially, beginning to explore their beliefs, values and choices. This moment is not understood as the beginning of an end (i.e. the transition to adulthood, independence or interdependence) but rather, as the beginning of a life long process of reflection, learning and growth.

There is a moment in people's lives, call it adolescence, when they embark on a new and often painful journey. That moment is different from what they have experienced before and different from what they will experience in the future. In that moment they begin to crystallise their upbringing and the beliefs and values that make them who they are. They are asking questions and they are searching for answers.

This is a particular moment of change – a moment that may include the psychological transitions and sociological pressures typically associated with adolescence. However, youth workers do not understand this as a transition ending in some enduring existence where, as adults, young people will no longer experience 'status ambiguity'; where their rights, roles and responsibilities are clear (Coleman, 1992); or where having a job, an independent household, marriage/cohabitation, parenthood and full citizenship will finally confirm their political, financial, social and sexual status as 'adults' (Morrow and Richards, 1996). Youth workers understand this moment in young people's lives as the beginning of a reflective process within which:

*The role of the youth worker is to recognise and nurture that process. We need to support young people to ask **their** questions and find **their** answers by enabling their reasoning and opening up their choices.*

It is a moment of questioning – a moment in which young people reflect critically on their sense of self, their beliefs and values. It is a moment that demands attention to enabling 'reasoning' and the opening up of options. Yet, whilst youth workers reject the 'transition theory' of young people's lives, this does not mean that they have no interest in the concept of 'adulthood'. From youth workers' perspectives:

Adulthood is a very individual thing but I think some of the common features would be people who are somehow at peace with themselves, having a sense of themselves and where their life is going, and a feeling of responsibility to themselves and others. The kind of self-respect that you get from feeling responsible for yourself and what you want to do with your life.

Adulthood is when you are able to make your own decisions and take control of what you want to do. Being able to say what you believe even if everyone else believes something different. Having enough personal confidence to be able to give to others. Being able to be in a group of your peers but be an individual. Accepting your responsibilities.

To me, the adult state is about the ability to engage in a clear exchange of information and being non-manipulative in the sense that it's not about playing games or trying to outdo somebody else or make them feel bad . . . [It's about] the way a person conducts their life. The way that they acknowledge where they are at and their feelings. The existence of a clear value system. Having one's own thoughts and desires. For a young person with a disability, it may be that they will never be financially independent, or will not necessarily have their own home. For some, they will always live in a system where there are carers or support workers. But that doesn't mean that they will also have an absence of a clear sense of self, independent thought and a worked out set of values. And in that sense, they have the potential to be as independent as the next person.

Adulthood means being in control of yourself, and the thing about being young is about feeling like 'I'm not in control of myself'. So you get this talk about pregnancy like it's this accident that happened. And I keep saying how can it be an accident? You were there. He was there. You engaged in sexual intercourse. That's not accidental. An accident is when you trip and fall down the stairs. The conception may be something that you didn't think would happen to you but the whole thing isn't accidental because you got to a point where you could have made a decision. So adulthood is the capacity to make decisions and choices based on the knowledge of the consequences for yourself, community and ultimately all that is; not placing the responsibility for your actions elsewhere. So saying your hormones are running away with you or you're under stress or you can't control your anger is reneging on the choices you made and your responsibilities. Adulthood is about having emotional maturity, control over yourself including your emotions.

The qualities and capacities, which these workers attribute to 'adulthood' therefore include:

- The ability to engage in a clear exchange of information without seeking to manipulate or 'outdo' others.
- Having self-respect and personal confidence.

- Taking responsibility for one's own actions.
- Making choices from an informed position having considered the consequences for yourself, the community and others.
- Being in control of your life and having a sense of where your life is going.
- Being able to be in a group of peers and still be an individual.
- Being able to say what you believe even if everyone else believes something different.
- Being able to give to others.
- Acknowledging where you are at – your feelings, thoughts and desires.
- Having emotional maturity and control of yourself including your emotions.
- Having a clear value system.

Interestingly, these qualities are neither age specific nor do they reflect the kinds of qualities and circumstances which Coleman (1992) and Morrow and Richards (1997), for example, identify as typifying the state of adulthood. There is no mention here of having achieved clarity regarding one's (social and political) rights, roles and responsibilities. No discussion of particular life events – e.g. leaving school, getting a job, leaving home, marriage, parenthood. No reference to the level of the political, legal, financial, social or sexual independence which adult status may be thought to confer.

'Maturity' and 'discipline'

Youth workers' understanding of 'adulthood' is, in fact, much more akin to Davies and Gibson's much earlier view of 'maturity' in the sense that it is:

> *A highly developed sensitivity to the requirements of others on oneself and a flexibility to express the appropriate aspects of one's individuality to meet the situation. Such maturity does not come rapidly and assumes the self-discipline and humility which comes from a careful discernment of one's own social situation and personal potentiality.*

> (Davies and Gibson, 1967: 94)

Indeed, Josephine Macalister Brew had much earlier referred to discipline as the 'system by which man achieves freedom and fits himself for carrying its responsibilities' (1943: 274). In this instance, discipline was conceived in terms of physical discipline (bringing the body under control) discipline of the emotions (mastering one's feelings so that emotions are not the reflex response of unexpressed fears), discipline of the mind (the educative discipline) and discipline of the spirit – best expressed in service to one's fellows and community (Brew, 1943: 274–5).

But again we have to be careful not to suggest that this mystical moment of 'youth' does not bring with it its own pressures, questions and concerns. For despite the difficulties we may experience with defining the concepts of 'adolescence', 'adulthood' and 'youth', it cannot be denied that there is a specific experience, or range of experiences, resulting from being young in Britain today – the reality of which young people themselves are only too aware:

Being a teenager is the worse part of your life – well so far anyway. There are so many things going round in your head that you're realising about people. Like when you're a child a smile is just a smile, but when you're older, when you're around your teenage years a smile is different. There's a malicious smile, a cheeky smile, a false smile, a genuine smile. All these things are entering into your head and that's just a smile and you've got four things already that you're not sure about. But it's just life. Everything. And for me being Asian in England is really hard. That was hard at school. It just seems like the world is really big. You don't realise how big it is. And there are so many hormones and emotions and all sorts of things that you don't know about and there are no answers for. It's terrible.

Adolescence seems to kind of defeat the purpose of childhood. I got to 16 and realised that I didn't really know what a childhood was because I thought, 'Was that my childhood?' Up to that point I'd been sheltered by school and a whole system. Then I got to 16 and thought 'Oh'. I think it's good that schools treat you more like an adult in your last year. It kind of prepares you. But the truth is you don't really know what you're doing. You just think you'll go on the dole. You just look for another system that you can secure yourself with. I think parents have to play a big role in that. They have to give you some of the independence that you need to grasp and experience. The funny thing is even though leaving school is a really big moment it doesn't really hit you until you're not there and you're thinking I'd be in maths now or I'd be getting told off now, I'd be wagging now. It doesn't hit you until then how sheltered you've been. How lenient they were and how secure the whole environment was. You don't realise until you're out of it all. I left school at 16 and I'd gone through the whole of those 16 years with someone telling me what to do. I felt lost when I left school.

I think youth workers have a really important role today because it's such a fast pace society. It's like the identity crisis. 'Who am I?' There are all these people around me. Different cultures, different languages, different religions. And there are more and more pressures on young people that are increasing the rate of distress like with eating disorders. But it isn't just about mental health. It's anything and everything to do with young people.

Nobody can judge what the next person can or cannot cope with. People are individual people. So for some people you won't even notice adolescence. But for others you will do. And what you see is that it's a time of confusion. It's an awful time because I'm going through it now and I'm asking myself all these questions like who am I, what is my role in society, where am I, where do I go, what is my status? And it's not just about who and what and where I am. It's about how you feel within yourself and how you feel about this glamour around you about being size ten. How do you feel about these ideals that you have to live up to? How do you feel about the fact that one day you're going to have to leave home and then your support just stops. And that's what contributes to distress within this society. Because you're moving away from the extended family and with new technology you are moving away all of the time and becoming more and more isolated.

Of course, there are all sorts of young people since they are, after-all, unique individuals who live in different circumstances, face different issues, have different interests, and aspire to different achievements. Young people are also different because some of them are women and others are men; they are Black or white; heterosexual, lesbian or gay; have a disability; come from a range of class backgrounds and religious commitments. Faced with such diversity it may appear that young people are not really 'a group' at all, since their identification as a social group requires the existence of some shared experience or quality. One is almost forced to ask, 'What is the common experience that young people share?' The answer to which is, of course, their age. Being *young* is the common experience that young people share.

Ageism

Whilst different young people may experience the psychological changes of 'adolescence' in different ways and to varying degrees, one consistent experience shared by them is the imbalance of power between young people and adults, which means that despite wanting to be shown respect, young people often feel that their views are not taken seriously (Coleman, Catan and Dennison, 1997). The issue of power, however, extends much further than the question of 'being taken seriously'.

Indeed, Franklin and Franklin (1990) identified three dimensions of *ageism* (cultural, political and economic) affecting both young and old people. Central to their argument was the understanding that 'power is not an attribute of individuals but an expression of a relationship between them' (Franklin and Franklin, 1990: 5). In addition:

Power is not always, although it can be, expressed in dramatic confrontations or battles between powerful individuals, classes, races or nations. It is more commonplace for power relations to become routinised within the life of a society so that overt opposition between dominant and subordinate groups is rare. The most effective exercise of power is a quiet affair in which individuals and groups may be ignorant of their subordination.

(Franklin and Franklin, 1990: 5)

Power relations are also never one-dimensional. The ageism experienced by young people may be intertwined with other forms of oppression deriving from their class, race, gender, sexuality or disability thereby 'creating a complex pattern of relationships of power and subordination' (Franklin and Franklin, 1990: 7).

The oppression of young people, therefore, shares a number of common features with other forms of oppression in the sense that it is:

- Systematic and structured.
- Based on stereotypes, prejudices and misconceptions.
- Operates at personal, cultural, and structural levels (Thompson, 1997).
- Leads to adverse representation of and discrimination against young people.
- Acts to exclude young people from aspects of social, political and economic life.
- Is underpinned by an ideology based on the inherent 'inferiority' of young people because of their age.

As Franklin and Franklin observe:

Ageism, like racism and sexism, expresses a power relationship between a dominant and subordinate group. The complex package of patronising and prejudicial views about young and old people which ageism embodies, justifies and sustains many of the injustices which these groups suffer.

(1990: 26)

So despite the social changes which mean that a significant minority of young people experience 'a wide range of problems and acute crises in adolescence' (Social Exclusion Unit, 2000), young people continue to be portrayed as a threat to society in terms of the social damage they may do through their irresponsible behaviour (e.g. in relation to sex, drugs and anti-social behaviour).

Indeed, Wyn and White observe that 'the popular image of young people presenting a 'threat' to law and order presents young people as more powerful than they really are' (Wyn and White, 1997: 12) – particularly since young people are both 'the symbol of society's future and its victims at risk of succumbing to lives of violence, drug dependence and moral degeneracy' (Wyn and White, 1997: 20).

That the term 'youth' has come to signify 'thugs' (car thieves, vandals, hooligans), 'users' (drugs, alcohol, smoking), and 'victims' (unemployment, poor schooling, dysfunctional families) (Jeffs and Smith, 1998) – none of which are categories, experiences or qualities specific to young people – creates compelling support for the argument that:

It is increasingly difficult to approach 'youth' as a meaningful way of categorizing a set of experiences or qualities . . . [and that since] . . . 'youth' is almost exclusively employed to signify discussion of a social problem or

*behaviour being portrayed in a negative light ... [youth work is] ...
entwined with a view of young people as being in deficit ... [and
therefore] ... the notion of youth work has a decreasing usefulness.*

(Jeffs and Smith, 1998: 50–61)

Yet whilst Jeffs and Smith's observations are well founded, young people's
experience of being young remains, specifically in relation to their search for
identity within the confines of the personal, cultural and structural ageism
which they encounter.

Resistance and collective action

So whilst it is certainly true that not all 'thugs, users and victims' are young,
it is equally true that young people, nonetheless, share a distinctive experience
of being young not least of which is the likelihood that being young increases
the chances of being labelled a 'thug, user or victim'.

Yet if 'youth' is deemed to be a problem in need of 'surveillance,
incarceration and control' as Jeffs and Smith have observed (1998), the
question is whether to dispense with the term or whether to reclaim it within
a framework of resistance in much the same way as we have reclaimed
'woman' and 'Black', and 'queer' by gay and lesbian activists (e.g. Woods,
1995), and 'nigger' by contemporary black film-makers (Pini, 1997).

This is not to suggest that such terms could possibly hope to convey the
richness and complexity of who we are as unique human beings. No single
term could. But, in a political sense, such terms act as signifiers offering
recognition to our experience and struggle in the face of the personal, cultural
and structural oppressions we encounter.

Understanding the experience of 'being young' in contemporary society
therefore lies at the heart of effective youth work. Naming 'youth' provides
a focus for young people's experience as *young people* thereby enabling them
to confront the contradictions and stereotypes of ageism; and create the
possibility for collective action.

Having examined 'adolescence' and 'youth' as central concepts for youth
work, we turn now to the question of young people's development as people.
That is:

- Their sense of themselves as human beings and members of particular
  social groups (**identity**).
- Their developing values and values system (**ethical standards**).

Identity

Identity represents a sense of self that includes a conscious sense of one's
individual uniqueness and a sense of solidarity with a group's ideals (Erikson,

1968). It embodies an understanding of how one is like all other people, like some other people and not like any other person (Gallatin, 1975 cited in Coleman and Hendry, 1999).

Erikson believed that 'identity crisis' was normative to adolescence and young adulthood in the sense that he saw the process of identity formation as emanating from the experience of some 'crisis'. The intention here, however, is not to cast young people's identity development as necessarily problematic, but rather, to acknowledge that entry into any new period of life involves challenges to an individual's self-concept. In other words, a person starts to ask themselves questions about the sort of person they are. This process involves self-reflection in terms of 'social comparison' (How am I like other people? What is my level of worth compared to others?), and exploration of personal values (Coleman and Hendry, 1999).

However, whilst such self-reflection occurs at different significant moments in the course of life, 'adolescence' represents the first phase of life during which the individual develops a clear personal and social identity that persists throughout life (Coleman and Hendry, 1999). This makes the issue of identity central to youth work as an age specific activity.

Also, while accepting the existence of shared patterns of identity development in young people it needs to be noted that the development of self-concept varies in relation to factors related to social background, whether this is in relation to personal circumstances (e.g. unemployment, family circumstances) or structural factors such as class, gender or race. Indeed, it has been argued that not only does 'race' affect identity development but also that young people from Black and white communities actually follow different pathways in becoming aware of their ethnic identity (Lorenz, 1996; Robinson, 1997). This asymmetry exists for social and political reasons because:

In the context of a racist society, feeling proud of being Black is not analogous to feeling proud of being White.

(Tizard and Phoenix, quoted in Lorenz, 1996: 160)

I think it's important for young people to be aware of their identity and to preserve that identity as best they can. My role in that is to enhance their identity and provide information to them. This is what they're asking for and I think as workers it's important that we support it. Not dilute it. This third and fourth generation have now started to call themselves British Muslims. Not Pakistani Muslims or Indian Muslims but British Muslims. That's a political statement that says they were born here. They didn't come from somewhere else. They belong here. They are British and they are Muslim.

But having a clear identity requires an understanding of what it means to be a Muslim. It's a question they have to ask themselves. What it means to them. I'm not there to judge whether they are good or bad Muslims. Nobody can do that. After all, you could have a humanist person who is caring and sharing and a non-Muslim and still a good person – a good human being. So the same thing goes with the Muslim. You could have someone who is praying five times a day and practising Islam but a good Muslim is what is inside oneself. It's about sharing and caring for other people. And that's really just like being a good human being. So first and foremost the issue is about being a good person.

At the same time, young people feel themselves to be different. They are concerned about who they are as part of a world wide Muslim community and what's happening around the world especially with the Muslims. They are concerned about it and some of them want to be known as Muslims. Others don't because they've seen that it has negative things connected with it. Like a few weeks ago in France there were teachers going on strike because the headmaster allowed a couple of young women to wear headscarves to attend school. The feeling among the young people was, 'Why are they doing this to us?' And the only reason they come up with is because we are Muslims and we have a different way of life. So the challenge for me as a youth worker is how to turn that into a positive. To look at how we can best contribute within this society that we live in – to contribute to this society as Muslims. Not as non-Muslims. Not as Pakistanis. Yes, young people are interested in visiting Pakistan or Bangladesh and even supporting the Pakistan cricket team. But what they are absolutely clear about is that they are staying here. They are a part of this country. And so they want to contribute to this society as Muslims and be accepted on their terms.

Within youth work, the development or preservation of identity is, therefore, not about judging young people but rather providing information and supporting them to understand what (for instance) being Muslim *means to them*. Indeed in discussing pedagogical principles in the development of anti-racist strategies, Lorenz comments that 'young people have to be facilitated in forming and expressing their ethnic identity, not in adopting given identities' (Lorenz, 1996: 161).

All my work with young Black people is about enabling them to develop an identity that makes them balanced and operational within this society. When we think of identity we may say that this person is a Black person or dual heritage or whatever concept or notion the European world places upon us as people they see as different. Our choice is to either accept or reject it. For me, one of the most negative aspects of having to embrace the term Black in this society is that it doesn't come with any cultural meaning. It's just a political term. It doesn't tell you anything about what it means to be Black in this society. So when a young person embraces this concept of being Black it becomes a tool that is used to remove them from their true identity. Black is a useful political term. But most other ethnic minority groups move away from that when they are not directly involved

*in the politics. So if you are from India you are Indian, or from China,
Chinese or wherever. You are an indigenous person from that part of the
globe. But for people particularly from the Caribbean and Africa that
concept of Blackness is something which defines us regardless.*

Also, whilst Tajfel observed that ethnic identity is 'that part of an individual's
self-concept which derives from their knowledge of their membership of a
social group (or groups) together with the value and emotional significance
attached to that membership' (Tajfel, quoted in Lorenz, 1996: 160), it is easy
to see the relevance of such a definition for other 'identities'. In other words
that being, for example, gay, or working class, or Jewish could equally be
described as 'that part of an individual's self-concept which derives from
his/her knowledge of his/her membership of a social group (or groups)
together with the value and emotional significance attached to that membership'.

The body 'inscribed'

But the 'fashioning of identity' is not merely a matter of being a man or
woman; Black or white since, as Foucault (1988) observed, it is not the
'physical body' which has meaning but the particular cultural and historical
contexts within which the meaningless body becomes 'raced' or 'gendered'.
It is the cultural and historical *context* rather than the body itself which gives
rise to meaning and therefore identity: a context within which 'bodies' have
already been 'coded' as a result of being classified and regulated by ourselves
and others. For example, in the way that the female body has been coded as
'hysterical', the Black body as 'deviant', the teenage body as 'rebellious', the
disabled body as 'invalid' (Pini, 1997: 158). For this reason, as one interviewee
observed:

> *The process of young people's growing self-identity and definition involves
> knowing not only 'who they are' but also 'who they are not'. That means
> sifting the messages that permeate the social system to understand what
> they are 'told' about who they are and making sense of this in the context
> of their own experiences, thoughts and feelings.*

Or, as expressed by Erich Fromm:

> *Unless I am able to analyse the unconscious aspects of the society in which
> I live, I cannot know who I am, because I do not know which part of me
> is not me.*

(1993: 78)

The process of their developing identity therefore forces young people to
confront the ways in which *their* body (and the bodies of others) has been
classified, 'inscribed' and regulated within the context of ageism, racism,

sexism, homophobia and other structural inequalities and institutionalised oppressions that operate. That is, the ways in which people are perceived and treated because they are, for example, women in a sexist society, Black people in a racist society or young people in an ageist society. For it is from within this context that young people engage in the process of 'making sense' of themselves, their lives and their world.

> Young people are influenced by their peers. But I think they are also searching for an identity or individuality that says I'm part of this group but I'm still that little bit different. We often talk about peer groups but we don't often talk about young people as individuals within that. And actually in any group you'll find a dynamic range of people who have a lot in common but also have a lot of things that are different about them.
>
> To me, racism represents ten to fifteen years of painful transition – years of explaining to your elders and arguing with your colleagues. I'm not sure it represents that for most young Black people today. So I understand the impact of what racism does to people not only from my own experience but also from the way young people understand it. And actually, because they did not experience that painful historical transition, they are much more confident about their ability to cope and deal with it. They have a sense of being able to play the system, work it, beat it, side-step it. And while I may not necessarily agree with young people's agenda on how to deal with these political issues, I have to accept that this is how they see it and how they experience it. Their attitude is very much 'this is how it is now, deal with it'. That makes them very much more pragmatic than I ever was.
>
> The importance of who you are, where you've come from and your roots is strongly grounded in our sense of community and continuity. Young people have that now. It's not necessarily something they had to discover. It's a way of life that goes without saying – a legacy that they've been given of right. So when you ask them to think about home and what goes on there and who their role models are they can tell you. That provides them with a platform from which to move on. When I listen to young adults or young people talk about it and the history of the people who they think made them, it really is awesome because they can stand proud without the tears and the pain. They can express their point without the emotion I had to keep bottled up. They can see a vision based on the black pearls of wisdom they were given as children and the history of our people which has informed them and given them self-belief in what they can do.

What becomes clear is that supporting young people to form and express their own identity, as opposed to adopting given identities, is a central part of the youth worker's responsibility not only in relation to ethnic identity but also in relation to other identities. In practice, this means providing opportunities for young people to develop both their self-image and self-esteem given that identity or self-concept involves a person's:

- Self-image – their description of self; or knowledge of membership of a social group(s).
- Self-esteem – their evaluation of self; or the value and emotional significance attached to membership of particular social group(s). (Coleman and Hendry, 1999)

Self-image *(Description of self)*

We often use residential week-ends and festivals to look at contemporary issues. The starting point is usually that week's reading from the Torah – which has been read out at synagogue. What we're asking is what contemporary issues can we draw from this? This becomes quite an astounding experience for the young people because they are confronted with the sense of their religious history and suddenly realise that it may hold some contemporary relevance or dilemmas for them.

My approach to young men's work is about creating opportunities in a relaxed atmosphere for young men to be more honest and open about themselves and all that comes from that. We have never dangled any carrots in order to get young men involved. We've always made it clear that if they come to the group they'll be expected to talk about themselves and explore what being young men means to them. The interesting thing is that when you create that opportunity to talk the hardest part is getting them to stop talking and listen to each other. It's just like the flood gates have opened because the opportunity is there, perhaps for the first time, to talk about themselves in a reflective rather than superficial way.

Self-esteem *(Evaluation of self)*

I see everyday in young Black people, in their negative behaviour, towards each other, how they have internalised the negative aspects of what this society deems as Black. So I very much see my role as helping young people to deconstruct that and look at what their Blackness means to them. What is it that's unique about being in their state of Blackness? What is unique about claiming their Africanity? And when you have tuned into that you can stand up as a more powerful person because you are defining who you actually are based on your knowledge of your history. If young Black people today haven't got that understanding of their history then they are very much confined to a notion of being Black or African as an insignificant thing – that we have never had any power as a race of people; that we have done nothing; that we have contributed nothing on the world platform; that we have no history; that our history began when the European came and enslaved us. It's all negative. Even the images they get of Africa today is very much about disadvantage, famine – all the negatives in society. So why would you want to associate yourself with that? The term Black becomes a problem because it is an easy option. You can exist in an aspect of Blackness even though it doesn't necessarily support who you actually are.

Once you can deal with that part of your personality which is you being gay it makes it easier to deal with other stuff – like stuff you may have about your parents of whatever. It's like once I realised I was gay, and even though I was completely chilled out about gay people and everything, I suddenly thought, 'Oh my God. I'm gay and I hate myself and I think I'm really ugly and I'm going to have a horrible life and I'm never going to meet anybody'. But once I started coming to the project and being with other gay people and all my friends knew then everything else didn't seem so bad. It seemed to fall into place.

Identity and moral orientation

Also, concepts of 'self' and morality are inextricably bound. In other words, I am my values. For example, referring to Taylor's exposition on the historical evolution of the modern concept of self, Crossley comments:

Taylor's contention is that concepts of self and morality, what he sometimes calls 'the good', are inextricably intertwined. He argues that we are selves only in that certain issues matter for us. What I am as a self, my identity, is essentially defined by the way things have significance for me. To ask what I am in abstraction from self-interpretation makes no sense (Taylor, 1989: 34). Moreover, my self-interpretation can be defined only in relation to other people, an 'interchange of speakers'. I cannot be a self on my own but only in relation to certain 'interlocutors' who are crucial to my language of self-understanding. In this sense, the self is constituted through 'webs of interlocution' in a 'defining community' (Taylor, 1989: 39). This connection between our sense of morality and sense of self, according to Taylor, means that one of our basic aspirations is the need to feel connected with what we see as 'good' or of crucial importance to us and our community. We have certain fundamental values which lead us to questions such as 'what kind of life is worth living?' and 'what constitutes a rich, meaningful life, as against an empty, meaningless one?'

(Crossley, 2000: 15)

Other 'self-theorists' have also cast 'virtue' (adherence to moral and ethical standards) at the top of the hierarchy of dimensions, which they refer to as *global self-esteem*. This includes:

- Competence or success in meeting achievement demands.
- Social acceptance, or attention, worthiness, and positive reinforcement received from significant others.
- Control or feelings of internal responsibility for outcomes.
- Virtue or adherence to moral and ethical standards. (Coleman and Hendry, 1999)

Interestingly, all of these aspects are needs, which have long been emphasised and addressed by youth workers.

Competence or success in meeting achievement demands

We have an accreditation system in our senior section. Most of this is about moving on. Young women get a certificate in relation to the eight personal development areas identified in the 'Look Wider' programme. Those areas are Out of Doors, International, Independent Living, Sport and Fit for Life, Leadership, Creativity, Service in the Community and Personal Values. When you are in the Guide section, 10–14, you do a selection of these. The words are different but they're the same eight things. When you get to be 14 plus you can specialise or have a particular focus that the unit is trying to work through.

I think it's pretty much accepted that class can adversely affect your success at school. So part of our role is to compensate by creating opportunities for young people to succeed. That's not saying that working class young people have more, or more important needs than middle class young people. I think it's just that the needs of the two groups are different. I have to admit though that middle class young people are more likely than working class young people to be able to sort out their own issues or problems. Or certainly that they tend to have more people and resources around them to help them sort out those things.

Social acceptance, or attention, worthiness, and positive reinforcement received from significant others

When we're talking about the development of social skills what we're often talking about is the kind of social skills that working class young people need to help them deal with people of a middle class background. Frequently, it's about gaining the confidence to engage with or deal with people in authority or people they think are more important than they are. So you are often in situations with them where you have to be saying: 'You're just as important as everybody else in this queue or everybody else trying to see this person. Don't put yourself down'. As a youth worker you have to find different ways of saying this but basically it's about getting young people to value themselves and have the confidence to believe they are as important as anybody else. When we are not directly addressing it we are doing so indirectly by encouraging young people to do things that increase their confidence and make them look important to others.

Taking a group of young people to Egypt helped that group of young people to shift their sense of self and their understanding of their people's contribution to the world stage. There was a level of pride and dignity that was nurtured within the group as they began to explore their connection with Egypt and their understanding of Egypt as an ancient and prominent civilisation. Young Black people need to be given experiences and encounters with Africa which can enhance their self-concept and develop a positive sense of self.

Control or feelings of internal responsibility for outcomes

I started off as a trouble-maker when I was a junior. Now I'm a volunteer leader at the junior club and I can see what I used to do. I can see the thing from both sides now. I'm lucky being on the leadership training programme because it makes me explore how I was although it's kind of scary because it has come around so quickly. But I've definitely changed as a person. I can criticise myself now as a leader and it helps me with communication and gives me a good experience because I love being with the little kids.

We are there to offer clarity and help young people understand the consequences of their actions. We provide a safe environment for them to deal with the conflicts of self that they may have.

Virtue or adherence to moral and ethical standards

The operating world view as it relates to practice is paramount within my approach to youth work. Young people of African heritage need to experience positive encounters with African culture as part of the journey, which aids the positive development of their identity. There need to be opportunities for young Black people to critically analyse their belief systems, enabling them to explore how their current beliefs are affecting their perception, cognition and knowledge. Contrasting the consequences of differing belief systems introduces alternatives for young people that lead to development and growth, leaving young people in the position of making conscious choices and accepting responsibility for them.

That volunteering has survived for young people is nothing short of a miracle given Thatcher's Britain in which the question that was always asked is, 'What's in it for me?' But I think the reason they've pulled through is partly because of their Jewish values and sense of community and continuity.

Morally textured landscape

In addition, since humans are, by nature, social beings, our identities are inevitably a function of our social relations. Therefore, in order to sustain our identities we must 'morally respect' both the identities of those around us, and the social relations which sustain those identities (Shotter, 1993). Indeed, according to Shotter, in order to qualify as citizens we must perceive ourselves as being in a 'morally textured landscape'. We must understand how we are currently 'placed or positioned' in that landscape and operate from an awareness that 'opportunities for action' are made differentially available because of our location (1993: 162).

Identity is therefore a question of morals. Not simply because virtue (adherence to moral and ethical standards) is a crucial dimension of self-esteem but because we are social beings living in a 'morally textured landscape': a landscape that requires us to understand our moral responsibility to ourselves and others; a landscape that requires us to develop, through our changing sense of self, a consistent set of values and the virtue that makes us authentic human beings.

Ethical standards

However, morality cannot be understood as a set of universally valid rules since moral action requires choices to be made – not simply in choosing whether to steal or not to steal; to lie or not to lie – but in the more complex weighing of one 'good' (e.g. loyalty) against another 'good' (e.g. justice). In the process of such deliberations, we come to recognise the necessity for rational judgement within a 'coherent system of precepts' (Williamson, 1997).

Youth work is not, therefore, concerned with the inculcation of a prescribed set of values, but rather, with the development of young people's:

- Critical skills and rational judgement.
- Disposition towards a 'coherent system of precepts', which underpin the exercise of such judgements.

In other words, youth work's intention is to enable and support young people to develop the critical skills and moral dispositions needed to make rational judgements and choices that they can sustain through committed action.

This is not, however, a solitary activity since:

The moral self is nurtured in social contexts and develops through learning and through being a member of and living within a society and making the moral decisions which are inescapably part of being a sentient human being.

(Williamson, 1997: 103)

Indeed, it is primarily through such social contexts that people are enabled to develop an understanding of their moral nature as human beings. Youth work can therefore be understood as the engagement of young people in the social contexts and deliberations, integral to their development as moral human beings – where morality is seen as being concerned with:

- Conduct in relation to people's well-being.
- Freedom of choice.
- Impartiality that applies equally to all persons in similar circumstances. (Barrow, 1981)

Clearly, this is not an easy task particularly given the constant tension between the needs of the individual and the needs of the 'state' – conceptualised by Aristotle in terms of whether education should:

- Develop the potential for excellence in each individual or their ability to serve the good of the *polis*;
- Promote the noblest life or the most comprehensive civic life; or
- Promote the education of the free citizen who is capable of deliberating while giving directions to those unsuited for self-rule. (Rorty, 1993: 35)

Not surprisingly, social education within youth work has always attempted to balance 'individual self-expression with a degree of conformity' (Davies and Gibson, 1967: 17) in the interest of the common good.

What I want is for young people to grow up to be responsible members of society and that they share and care. The reason that they should share and care is because it works. It's basically the Christian message. Love your neighbour as yourself. Society will work but you need to give a bit. It's actually the very opposite of the enterprise culture with which we are now all imbued and which says, 'What are you volunteering for? Aren't you good enough to get paid?'

A residential is the best place to think about how you treat other people – which is basically where all values start because it's no good having wonderful global values about equal opportunities if you can't get on with the people around you. It is also an important place for young people to learn to be in control. It's a chance for them to come out of their norms into a different set of norms. Very often it's a chance for them to feed themselves. And that's quite a big thing for young women today because most of them don't actually do a lot of cooking at home. Then there's the activities and all the social time which is when the conversations really happen – around preparing the meal, eating it and all the other things that have to be done.

However, while some would argue that not all values are moral values they are all, nonetheless, based fundamentally on some conception of what is 'right' or what is 'good'. Or as Milton Rokeach put it 'an enduring belief that a specific mode of conduct or end state of existence is personally or socially preferable to an opposite or converse mode of conduct or end state of existence'(1973: 5). In other words, that telling the truth, for example, is preferable to lying or deliberately misleading others as a 'mode of conduct'. And that justice, for example, is preferable to injustice as 'an end state of existence'.

The challenge for youth work is how to develop a practice that:

- Addresses values without 'imposing' them;
- Maintains a meaningful and appropriate concern for individual as well as societal needs;
- Enables young people to engage in 'moral inquiry'; and
- Supports young people's disposition towards virtue:
  - as a central dimension of their self-esteem; and
  - as social beings in a morally textured landscape.

Values without 'imposition'

Engaging with young people in their social education is a privilege and a luxury. So you have to be very careful that you don't impose your own standards and values on them. That's where it becomes really skilful because you can't deny your own beliefs and values. But if you acknowledge them and are aware of where you are coming from then you stand a better chance of working effectively from your value base without imposing your view on young people.

For a long time now the youth service has been conscious of not wanting to just pass on a prescribed set of values. Yet at the same time we talk about youth workers being role models. The thing is young people don't choose as role models people who have no values or principles. They choose people they can identify with and that's often based on some moral or spiritual quality they respect. In fact, one of the most common things that African Caribbean, African, Asian young people have is some sort of faith or spiritual involvement that comes from their home and culture. It doesn't matter what religion the young people are. It's about faith and a belief in something that underpins the way they live their life and makes them as a person.

The individual and society

Most of the time people think that the universe is miles out there. But the truth is that you can go in and in and in as much as you can go out and out and out. Everything in the universe is connected. All the things we think of as being out there and all the things we think of as being in here. They are all connected. Some scientist said that in your lifetime every individual on earth is likely to breathe a cell of Jesus. And if you think about it when you sneeze millions of cells of your body are propelled into the universe and some cells are immutable, they just go up into the air and are carried on the stratosphere and drop down somewhere else. And they become part of everything else. So if you drop a piece of litter you make that area unpleasant. But if you didn't drop it and your friend sees you put the litter in your pocket instead you will have set an example and your friend might do the same. And in that moment you will have changed the universe. So I think what we are really about is changing the universe.

I was originally trained in religious life as a Franciscan friar and my basic philosophy when I came into youth work was the principle of the Franciscans – that basically all you need to do to get to Heaven is to keep the Commandments and love your neighbour: don't pinch his things and take responsibility. If you want to do something else Jesus said, 'Go and give all you have to the poor and come and follow me'. The Franciscans take that to mean 'Do what I do'. So as a youth worker my message to young people is that we don't need to know anything else to be happy. Love your neighbour, take responsibility and basically give. And the more you give the more you'll get.

Christian values are not the values just of Christians. They are the values that Christ put over to us. People sometimes mix that up because what has happened is that different individuals and groups have taken what Jesus said and changed and adapted it to suit their own interests – particularly in terms of power. What Jesus said was, 'This is the way we should behave as individuals to make a better society'. That is not the same as the values of the Church that has tortured people, had wars and done a whole load of other things.

Moral inquiry

One of the most basic Jewish values is to question your surroundings. A good illustration of this is a part of Jewish religious Law called the 'Mishna'. This is where you have a piece of text from the Torah in the middle of the page surrounded by eight to ten commentaries from different sources; some of them agreeing with each other, some completely disagreeing. There is page after page of this and the premise is that all these commentaries are right. In fact, in orthodox Jewish seminaries they sit from eight in the morning to eight at night, day after day, arguing over the same piece of text. Debate is seen as a very good thing.

Most young people do not know what they believe, morality and ethics are not curriculum subjects at GCSE. They behave in a way that is part of a group but when you ask them what do you actually believe they find it hard to express. For example, a young woman may not know that she values life and therefore disagrees with abortion until she is actually pregnant and faced with the dilemma of 'do I have an abortion or carry on with the pregnancy?' If this is the point at which she discovers that she does not agree with abortion then it could be said that she has no choice in the matter. Whereas, if she knew beforehand that she values life she may have taken greater responsibility of her reproductive powers and viewed that aspect of her creativity as sacred and therefore taken precautions so as not to get pregnant. So what youth work can do is help young people put their beliefs and values to the test in a safe way.

Disposition towards virtue

Whilst it has always been the case that some commitments to virtue arise from specifically religious values, Barrow maintains that '*good* exists independently of God and therefore morality does not depend on religion for its existence' (1981: 144). Therefore, people should engage in moral behaviour for its own sake, not out of fear or self-interest, or because we have been told to do so.

Virtues and virtue

Virtues refer to *particular* moral qualities for example, wisdom, courage, benevolence, compassion or trustworthiness. By contrast, virtue is 'an ethically admirable *disposition* of character [which] helps to determine, in the right contexts, what one will want to do' (Williams, 1993: 9). Virtue therefore requires that a person will choose to act in certain ways based on a disposition towards certain ideals. Virtue asks not 'What should I do?' but 'What would the just or compassionate or trustworthy or courageous or 'virtuous' person do?'

The practice of virtue therefore requires the ability to make judgements and take action whilst being guided by some underlying set of values or ethical principles – whether these have their origins in specifically religious beliefs, are considered to be part of an innate moral reality (See Confucius, trans., 1979) or the result of 'pure reason' (See Kant, trans., 1948).

Religious traditions

Something that's specific to young Jewish people, and perhaps other religious groups, is the sense of a life cycle. There is an annual Jewish cycle, a monthly, a weekly cycle, a daily cycle for some and it's very specific. A lot of young Jewish people have this as a value but they are not conscious of it because they have never known anything else. So for example they will know that every September is the New Year, whether they observe it or not. They know Friday and Saturday is Shabbat. Whether they choose to go out on a Friday night or choose to observe Shabbat they know it exists and they know it is significant because they are Jewish. There is Bar Mitzvah which is a very significant event whether they choose to observe it or not – and most of them do. All of this provides 'markers' that affect their values because life is not just one long thing. In that sense, they are used to being 'boundaried'. And whether they choose to observe it or not they know that boundary is there and fundamentally affects their lives.

Some people would say that there are no specifically Jewish values – just human values. But I think the Jewish take includes continuity. So the average, intelligent, questioning aware human being who wants to question themselves and their actions and the actions of other people – if that person is Jewish – also has another layer of religious understanding of themselves as part of a continuum which recognises those who went before and those who will come after. This is absolutely lodged in the Jewish unconscious. At 16 or 17 young people are becoming aware of this and their role in the Jewish community as part of the Jewish chain. So we get a lot of young people, and adults, who want to be volunteer workers because, in their words, they want to put something back into the community. And even though they may not identify it in a conscious way, it is still a recognition of the Jewish life cycle and the significance of continuity.

Within Judaism the pursuit of virtue rests on the imitation of God since God is good and therefore to be good is to be like Him:

> *Since human beings are created in the image of God, it is obvious that one achieves the highest possible level of perfection or self-realisation by becoming as similar to God as humanly possible. This is the basis of what may be the single most important ethical doctrine of the Hebrew Bible, that of imitatia Dei, the imitation of God ... One achieves holiness [that is] by obeying God's commandments or ... by walking in his ways.*

(Kellner, 1993: 84)

For Christians it is a case of obeying God's commandments whilst 'walking in the ways' of Jesus Christ – of showing forgiveness, loving kindness, mercy, compassion, charity, justice, faith, and most important, humility. However, the Golden Rule – 'do unto others as you would have them do unto you' – is not simply a command to follow some specific rule, but rather a requirement to think and deliberate about what each situation demands (Preston, 1993).

So whilst religions have established rules or principles of ethical behaviour – for example the Judeo-Christian Ten Commandments, the Buddhist Noble

Eightfold Path, the Five Pillars of Islam – it is also clear that the development of virtue is considered to rest not only on devotion to some greater wisdom, but also on the exercise of human reason.

> While revealing his will to humankind in the Quran, God also urges them to exercise reason in understanding revelation. Like Judaism and Christianity, Islam's beginnings are [thus] rooted in the idea of the divine command as a basis for establishing moral order through human endeavour.
>
> (Nanji, 1993: 107)

Indeed, whilst the Noble Eightfold Path contains within it a wide range of sanctions and prohibitions covering all aspects of human life and conduct, it is in essence a threefold scheme of moral training, which consists of:

- The development of wisdom – right understanding, right thought.
- The practice of virtues – right speech, right conduct, right livelihood.
- The practice of meditation – right effort, right mindfulness, right contemplation.

Thus, in Buddhist ethics there is a: . . . close integration of the ethical as a rational engagement of analysis and argument, as a normative recommendation of conduct and a way of life, as a social expression and as an intense personal quest and mode of character development (De Silva, 1993: 59).

Natural moral order

> There are two kinds of morality. We have laws in society, which set a kind of morality and we have conscience. I believe that conscience is innate. That is, you come into the world knowing all and you lose it through the processes we go through. But that inner morality is not a set of rules to follow. It is a recognition of the sacredness of life and our relationship to everything as complementary.

Confucius, believing in a natural moral order, subscribed to the ancient Chinese conception of Tao – The Way – the sum total of truths about the universe and humanity in the form of the individual and society. For Confucius virtue (Te) was scripted in Heaven to be cultivated by human beings. Confucian virtues include benevolence, wisdom, courage (when guided by morality), trustworthiness and righteousness although Confucius believed that 'the only worthwhile thing a man can do is to become as good a man as possible' (trans., 1979: 12).

Similarly, Mencius postulated that all people are born with four incipient tendencies in 'germ' or seed form – compassion which is the germ of benevolence; a sense of shame the germ of dutifulness; courtesy and modesty the germ of observance of the rites, and right and wrong the germ of wisdom (Mencius trans., 1970: 82). For Mencius, these four 'germs' constitute the 'original heart', which must be cared for, nurtured and cultivated in order to grow to full maturity. The purpose of the heart is to think and it is this, according to Mencius, which distinguishes human beings from animals. Therefore through our own effort human beings can perfect our own moral characters.

Also, like his teacher Plato, who believed in an unchanging unwritten 'law' to which all human behaviour is subject, Aristotle was also committed to natural justice 'which has the same authority everywhere, and is independent of opinion' (Aristotle trans., 1987: 167). Aristotle also believed that virtue lies in the degree to which 'reason' is or is not the ruling faculty in a person's being:

> *It is perfectly clear that it is the rational part of man which is the man himself, and that it is the virtuous man who feels the most affection for this part.*

(Aristotle trans., 1987: 309)

However, while producing an extensive catalogue of virtues (including courage, temperance, wisdom and justice), Aristotle considered justice to be the supreme virtue:

> *Justice ... is not a part of virtue but the whole of virtue; its opposite, injustice not a part of vice but the whole of vice.*

(Aristotle trans., 1987: 146)

Therefore the virtue of justice was considered to underpin all other virtues as well as provide the basis for deliberation and 'right reason'. And while Gilligan's (1982) theory of an ethic of care maintains that men (more so than women) conceive of morality as being based on justice whereas women (more so than men) conceive of morality as being based on caring for others, the reality is that every moral decision contains not only principle but also a context which, by its very nature, includes specific circumstances and relationships. Therefore taken together an ethic of justice and an ethic of care create a conception of morality within which:

> *The moral person is seen as one whose moral choices reflect reasoned and deliberate judgements that ensure justice be accorded each person while maintaining a passionate concern for the well-being and care of each individual.*

(Brabeck, 1993: 48)

So whilst some conceptualise virtue from a specifically religious base and others subscribe to an innate or natural moral order in the universe, both perspectives affirm the need for human beings to think and deliberate about what each situation demands and to exercise human reason.

In other words, the development of virtue requires the exercise of practical reason and rational judgement by autonomous human beings – that is people capable of acting in accordance with reason and from their own free will, voluntarily as opposed to acting 'under compulsion or from ignorance' (Aristotle trans., 1987: 66).

Practical reason

As a child you often accept your parents' view of the world. And that view is really the conclusion that they have come to about life. Then as you get older you start to test out, with other people, the views you've acquired from home to see whether they are right or real . . . So if they [young people] are saying to me that they want to be a positive person who contributes to society then what they have to understand is how their actual behaviour in different situations fits in with this helpful, kind, sharing person that they say they want to be. The issue becomes one of consistency; trying to develop a consistent sense of self in terms of their core attitudes, values and beliefs. Then when they make decisions about what is right or wrong, and these may be tough decisions, they are able to make them because they have a consistent set of values that enable them not only to make the decision but also to implement it. So their values provide a guide in terms of the things they would do as well as the things they couldn't possibly see themselves doing.

The foremost advocate of 'pure reason', Immanuel Kant, postulated that a good will is the only unconditioned good, and the purpose of reason is to produce a will that is good in itself as opposed to a will that is good as a means to something else.

Kant's categorical imperative was that people should 'act only on that maxim through which you can at the same time will that it should become a universal law' (i.e. *will* that everyone should behave in the same way). In other words, if I believe that it is OK for me to steal then (as a universal law) I must also be prepared to accept (or will) that it is OK for you to steal . . . and OK for you to steal from me. Kant's categorical imperative is therefore not a prescription for behaviour but a principle to be used in making rational moral judgements.

Also, since a rational person is one who acts in accordance with principles then, according to Kant, one reasons one's way to morality through the exercise of practical reason, or in other words through one's will (Kant trans., 1948).

Benn and Peters (1959) suggest that Kant's categorical imperative is actually underpinned by three principles:

- Impartiality – that is, impartial consideration of people as sources of needs, claims and interests.

- Respect for people as rational human beings – as illustrated in Kant's subordinate maxim 'treat humanity, whether in your own person or in the personal of any other, never simply as a means, but always at the same time as an end' (Kant trans., 1948).
- Autonomy – 'act as if you were through your maxims a law-making member of a kingdom of ends' (Kant trans., 1948) which, according to Benn and Peters (1959), demonstrates Kant's commitment to individual autonomy that also takes account of others' like moral status.

However, utilitarian philosophers dispute the idea that morality could be based on pure reason, for them, a thing can only be good if it is good for someone. Actions are therefore perceived as right or wrong according to the extent to which they promote the greatest good for the greatest number – usually construed as the greatest pleasure or happiness (See Bentham, 1948); in other words according to their consequences as opposed to their motive. But, deciding between our own happiness and that of others requires impartiality, and so utilitarianism requires the basic principle of benevolence (Benn and Peters, 1959).

Even by the utilitarian code then, one is still required to make some judgement about what would constitute the greatest good however construed. Therefore, utilitarianism requires not only benevolence but also some level of practical reason and rational judgement by autonomous human beings regardless of whether the motive is to exercise virtue for its own sake, or to bring about some particular consequence – i.e. the greatest good for the greatest number.

So the question becomes:

> . . . *not simply how am I to conduct myself in my life, but how am I to become the kind of person readily disposed so to conduct myself, the kind of person for whom proper conduct emanates characteristically from a fixed disposition.*
>
> (Kosman, 1980: 103)

And this brings us to the question of how people learn to be virtuous.

Learning to be virtuous

According to social psychologists Piaget (1932) and Kohlberg (1981; 1983) the process of moral development comes in a sequence of overlapping stages both cognitive and emotional during which young people learn to structure the way they think about rules and moral issues.

According to Piaget, the process is represented by a transformation away from a situation where rules are given by an external authority to a situation where rules are consciously deliberated and negotiated by the individual.

Kohlberg describes the process as a transformation from obeying rules through fear of punishment to seeking to establish universal principles through one's own experience and critical thought.

The process is therefore understood as moving beyond simple habituation to a concern not only with the existence of certain rules, but more centrally, with the general principles on which these rules are based.

In every family there are those pearls of wisdom. The maxims you were constantly being told by your parents. As adults we often think that young people ignore them. But I don't think that's true. I think young people hold on to the same pearls of wisdom that their parents gave them – even if they're just lodged in their minds. And those principles form the key elements that make up their life. What they are searching for is a way to move on from there. Perhaps discarding some of those pearls and establishing new ones or new interpretations that match their lives and the person they want to be as a part of this society. What they want is to please their parents, carers, and the people to whom they are accountable while also feeling valued and valuable. But what makes them valued to a parent isn't necessarily what makes them valued to a peer. So they struggle. A youth worker has to take all of this on board.

Young people are aware of the confusions and contradictions of life. What they are trying to do is put together a jigsaw puzzle without the picture on the box. They may even have a lot of the pieces but they still feel that they are not doing it properly. They are searching for some answers. For instance, their family may go to church and they themselves may be holding on to some of those beliefs. Yet, at the same time, they may be doing all sorts of things that are against what their family thinks. When you talk to them they might say that they believe in the Bible. They'll tell you: 'OK I never read it and I don't go to church but it doesn't mean I disregard it. Just because I don't use it in the way you want me to use it (youth worker, or mother or church leader) doesn't mean that I don't regard it.' The issue is not about judging young people or their actions. It's about listening to them and understanding how they are using the knowledge, ethical principles, beliefs and values they have acquired to inform their own lives.

However, in order to utilise 'knowledge, ethical principles, beliefs and values' to inform one's life one must necessarily be capable of making reasoned judgements. This is the basis of autonomy, not only in the sense of freedom of will, or regard for the like moral status of others, but also in terms of:

- An attitude to authority and 'taken for granted' rules that, though respectful of them, becomes increasingly questioning of the principles behind the rules.

- An increasing integration of the values and purposes that permeate one's actions and relationships.
- A sense of one's own value and identity through different circumstances and pressures. (Pring, 1984: 5)

The argument, following Dewey (1961), is that while people may inherit certain moral principles from their family and community they can nonetheless 'through rational inquiry, devise new solutions to social problems, working consciously together to reform their community and their own moral outlooks' (Schneewind, 1993: 154).

Being second or third generation African-Caribbean or African in this country means that the connection, traditions and values that perhaps their parents or grandparents had are now being recreated and coming up in a new format for the young people today. That can be both a good and a bad thing because obviously culture is always evolving therefore it's a moving thing and not a stagnant thing. So when I see young people re-asserting a Black culture and identity in a way that's different from how young people asserted it when I was young I think that's a good thing. But what can be lost in that are the core values from which your culture is derived. And I think sometimes it's the core values that help maintain you as a person when there's chaos and mayhem going on around you. If your values are sure then that supports any kind of choices in life that you seek to make.

I know the damage that has been done to Black people in thinking that we have to change or assimilate our values because European values and white middle-class values are somewhat better than ours. So concepts of parenting and all the other values that we came with have somehow been dissipated into a place where there are no boundaries for young people. Some people see that as liberating but I truly feel that for you to feel secure in this society you have to be held – not in a cage – but something that is holding you and supporting you. I don't see being ultra liberal as support. I see it as being negligent in fact. Because in order for us to feel whole and operate effectively we need to go through a process of understanding not only our rights but also our responsibilities and our connection to humanity.

Right action and right motive

There are therefore two basic issues of virtue:

- How to find right action in particular circumstances; and
- How to act from right motive. (Preston, 1993)

Finding right action

Central to 'finding right action' is the ability to make reasoned choices and yet, as Barrow observes:

> No doubt for many of us, much of the time, the reasons that lie behind our actions are muddled, insufficiently worked out or only vaguely formulated in our minds. Nonetheless we choose to act in some ways rather than others and our choices are based on reason – for to make a choice is precisely to opt for one thing rather than another for some kind of reason.
>
> (Barrow, 1975: 21)

Finding right action therefore requires the individual, firstly, to accept that they have choices, however limited or constrained; and secondly, be able to *make* choices based on reasoned and rational judgement. This is a continuous lifelong process since virtue is not:

> ... an eternal quality of an unchanging good human being, but a disposition of character that is able to select and practice the good within the recognition that authenticity of action is related to multiple dimensions of selfhood and self-transcending behaviour.
>
> (Streng, 1993: 98)

Finding right action is also a process nurtured in social contexts and therefore, in order to discover and develop authentic virtuous expression two conditions are needed:

1. A process of dialogue between sincere people who represent different ideologies – with each participant in the dialogue attempting 'to evoke the best, the deepest, the most enlightening aspects of the dialogue partner's orientation . . . instead of looking for ways to discredit it'.
2. The learning and cultivation of virtuous expression by practice as well as by testing and exploring in dialogue. (Streng, 1993: 99–100)

Indeed, it was Aristotle who commented that 'it is not enough to know the nature of virtue; we must endeavour to possess it, and to exercise it, and to use whatever other means are necessary for becoming good' (Aristotle trans., 1987: 351).

In this sense, 'dialogue' is envisaged not so much as a Socratic question and answer interrogation designed to uncover 'universal truths' but more as a 'conversation' in which young people are supported to know what *they* think, by being able to 'see' what they say (Weick, 1995). In other words, it is a conversation that involves mutual respect and freedom of rationality.

However, as Midgley observes:

> Discussing – serious, open-minded discussing rather than just disputing – is not easy. It is something that people need to learn to do while they are still

young and flexible ... that discussion is inevitably philosophical. Philosophy, in fact, is not a luxury. At least in confusing times like ours, philosophy is an unavoidable necessity.

(Midgley, 1997: 38)

Acting from right motive

However, acting from right motive is not merely a question of dialogue and reflection. Acting from right motive requires attention to feelings as well as thought, for as David Hume argued morality 'must be rooted in our feelings since morality moves us to action, and reason alone can never do so' (cited in Schneewind, 1993: 150). Indeed, as one worker remarked:

Maliciousness, downright cruelty, racism – and OK this sounds all pat – racism, sexism and so on, but I am quite serious. If someone makes a racist remark when we are in the minibus then there's no real discussion. That's out of line. It's unacceptable. You will not do that. You will not shout racist remarks out of the minibus. And then, after you've done that bit, then it's time for talking. There are times when values are very straight-forward.

The nature of youth work

The assertion here is therefore twofold:

- Firstly, young people's 'personal and social development' necessarily involves the question of *identity*. This is because youth workers engage with people at a particular point in their lives, a period typically known as adolescence, which we have for long acknowledged as a time of 'increased emotional awareness and spiritual or idealistic development' (Brew, 1957: 18). It is a time for 'exploring the boundaries of freedom', examining 'how one sees oneself and is seen by others' and reflecting on 'personal identity' (Leighton, 1972: 54). The intention here is not to cast young people's identity development as somehow problematic but rather to acknowledge that 'youth' has implications for youth work; and that central to 'youth' is the issue of identity.
- Secondly, questions of identity: 'Who am I?'; 'What sort of person am I?' are inextricably bound to the question of *personal values* 'What do I believe to be right or wrong/good or bad?' This, in turn, is related to self-esteem insofar as self-esteem arises not only from a sense of competence, worthiness and internal control but also, and importantly, from adherence to moral and ethical standards.

Therefore, if the purpose of youth work is to support the personal and social development of young people, at that particular moment in their lives, then this necessarily involves attention to their *moral development* in terms of their:

- Identity (self-image and self-esteem); and
- Personal values (specifically in relation to their adherence to moral and ethical standards).

As a result, it is in the *nature* of youth work to engage with young people in the process of moral philosophising through which they make sense of themselves and the world. As such, youth work is a process of reflection and self-examination through which young people increasingly integrate their values, actions and identity; and take charge of themselves as empowered human beings. Youth work therefore enables and supports young people to:

- Explore their values.
- Deliberate on the principles of their own moral judgements.
- Make reasoned choices and informed decisions that can be sustained through committed action.

Through this process of moral philosophising young people learn and develop:

- The skills of critical thinking and rational judgement.
- The ability to engage in 'moral inquiry' – about what is 'good' and conducive to the 'good life' generally – the ability which Aristotle called the development of practical wisdom.
- A disposition towards virtue (adherence to moral and ethical standards) – as a central feature of their identity and their responsibility as social beings in a social world.

This philosophical inquiry occurs through 'conversation' and the cultivation of virtuous expression through practise. As a part of this:

> It is important to destroy the wide-spread prejudice that philosophy is a strange and difficult thing just because it is the specific intellectual activity of a particular category of specialist or of professional and systematic philosophers. It must be first shown that all men (sic) are philosophers.
>
> (Gramsci, 1971: 9)

Summary

This chapter addressed the question of what youth work *is* – that is, its nature and is core purpose. It proposes that youth work is essentially concerned with supporting young people's growth and development 'as people'. That is, their development as human beings. However, given that youth work addresses itself to young people at a particular period in their lives, then understanding the concept of 'youth' becomes essential to understanding the purpose of youth work. In other words, youth work is about *young* (age range of target group) *people* (focus of development).

'Adolescence' and 'youth'

The concepts of 'youth' and 'adolescence' are discussed noting that whilst young people have different experiences of 'being young' because of their different social backgrounds, personal circumstances and structural factors in society; it is nonetheless the case that 'being young' gives rise to a shared experience of imbalance of power between young people and adults. This ageism is the oppression of young people *because they are young*. As such, it shares a number of common features with other forms of oppression in the sense that ageism is:

- Systematic and structured.
- Based on stereotypes, prejudices and misconceptions.
- Operates at personal, cultural, and structural levels (Thompson 1997).
- Leads to adverse representation of and discrimination against young people.
- Acts to exclude young people from aspects of social, political and economic life.
- Is underpinned by an ideology based on the inherent 'inferiority' of young people because of their age.

The contention here is that the term 'youth' acts as a political signifier offering recognition to young people's experience and struggle in the face of the personal, cultural and structural ageism they encounter. Understanding the experience of 'youth' therefore lies at the heart of effective youth work. Naming 'youth' provides a focus for young people's experience as *young people* thereby enabling them to confront the contradictions and stereotypes of ageism; and create the possibility for collective action.

Development as a person

In the process of their growth and development young people necessarily develop *their identity* (as individuals and members of particular social groups), and given the fundamental link between identity and moral orientation, a *set of ethical standards*, which guide and inform their choices and actions in the world.

These ethical standards are not universal rules to be followed but rather a set of moral principles which guide the choices to be made. For whether 'greater wisdom' is thought to come from one's God, or some natural moral order in the universe, virtue is nonetheless achieved through human endeavour. That is to say, virtue requires the exercise of practical reason. Human beings must deliberate about what they think they *ought* to do; and make judgements about what they will actually do. The development of virtue therefore involves a process of reflection through which individuals perfect their own moral character.

Youth work is not, therefore, concerned with the inculcation of a prescribed set of values, but rather, with the development of young people's:

- Critical skills of deliberation and rational judgement; and
- Disposition towards a coherent system of precepts, which underpin the exercise of such judgements.

This process of moral deliberation or inquiry is not, however, a solitary activity but one that takes place in social contexts. That is, contexts that involve both 'conversation' (deliberation), and the cultivation of virtuous expression through practise.

Nature and purpose

As such, the core purpose of youth work is to engage with young people in the process of moral philosophising through which they make sense of themselves and the world, increasingly integrate their values, actions and identity, and take charge of themselves as empowered human beings.

Youth work therefore enables and supports young people to:

- Explore their values.
- Deliberate on the principles of their own moral judgements.
- Make reasoned choices and informed decisions that can be sustained through committed action.

In the process, young people learn and develop the skills of critical thinking and rational judgement; the ability to engage in 'moral inquiry'; and a disposition towards virtue as a central feature of their identity and responsibility as social beings in a social world.

Chapter 3

Practice

Youth work, as defined in the previous chapter, engages young people in the process of moral philosophising as a function of their identity formation and development of ethical standards. This does not mean having a fixed set of values or code of behaviour into which young people are to be initiated or inculcated. Philosophical pursuit necessarily involves reflection and questioning. Neither does it suggest that such an endeavour can be achieved primarily through engagement in structured exercises about imagined situations since the development of identity, the construction of the person, takes place not only through one's own agency but also through interaction with others.

> *As what people say and do is always open to criticism and judgement by others, an essential part of being free individuals in a modern society, is them being able to justify their actions to others when required to do so – they require a capacity to be able to articulate 'good reasons' for their conduct. For, in executing their own actions, in acting as free agents (and in qualifying for their status as such), people cannot just act as they please, when they please. They must also act with a certain kind of socially shared awareness.*

(Shotter, 1993: 162)

The development of identity is, therefore, not an insular activity. As such, and in order to engage with young people, youth workers must make *relationships* with young people that enable them to develop the critical skills and moral dispositions needed to engage in the youth work *process*. That is, a process, which helps young people to make sense of themselves and their experiences and, in so doing, give meaning to their lives.

That is, relationships that involve:

- Accepting and valuing young people.
- Honesty, trust, respect and reciprocity.

And a process that involves young people in:

- Developing the skills of critical thinking and rational judgement.
- Participating in deliberations about what is 'good' – not only in particular respects, but in terms of what is conducive to the good life generally.

- Taking charge of their lives as empowered individuals as opposed to powerless victims – that is as rational human beings able to 'understand and act on the personal, social and political issues which affect their lives, the lives of others and the communities of which they are a part' (NYB, 1991: 16).

Central to the youth work process is a commitment to supporting young people to learn from their experience and 'make sense' of their lives through 'conversation' (Jeffs and Smith, 1999a) since 'talk, in the form of narratives, stories, accounts and so on, interprets what actions mean and thereby performs an evaluative function (Marshak, 1998: 21); and also because it is through narrative that 'people organise their experience in, knowledge about, and transactions with the social world' (Bruner, quoted in Cortazzi, 1993: 1).

Relationships

Moral education is a matter of becoming a certain kind of person – of coming to care in certain kinds of ways and this is not directly achievable by means of syllabi and classroom techniques of the familiar kind. As much as anything, the development of virtue is a function of the relationships within which people move, and which provide a context for whatever moral reflection they engage in.

(Kleinig, 1982: 253)

The relationship is everything because personal growth, development, learning about values are human tasks that can only be done within a relationship. Actually, the relationship is not only a base for sharing values but also the environment within which young people construct their sense of self – a model of themselves if you like, that they re-form and re-shape as they further explore and develop. Specifically in the Christian context the whole idea of an incarnate God is a central theme, which speaks of *being with* and *sharing* with as a means by which people test the validity and accuracy of their values.

So youth work provides opportunities in safe environments for young people to challenge and be challenged in order to learn about themselves, their relationship to their immediate community, their relationship to the world and their relationship to their God.

Youth workers must therefore be able to initiate and develop relationships of trust and mutual respect with young people, which motivate them to understand and develop their values. At the same time, young people need to feel safe enough to be open to sharing what they think and feel in order to enter into that sort of relationship. Of course, this all takes time. Values are deeply personal so the worker needs to keep focused on the young person and not be side-tracked by the benefits that they may see for some other party be it the church or society in general.

Relationships are, and always have been, at the heart of youth work. As such they represent one of the most consistent themes in youth workers' accounts and other descriptions of the work. Relationships are important because it is within the context of 'being with' and 'sharing with' others that people are supported to create and re-create themselves, take charge of their relationships (with self and others), actively engage in their community and contribute to the world. This requires trust, mutual respect, safety and time.

> *The relationship between the youth worker and young person is like the foundation of a house. If it's not firmly established then the walls and ceiling will collapse. There is a responsibility on the youth worker to demonstrate to young people that positive relationships with adults are possible. They also need to use opportunities to be positive role models for young people and put a human face on the values that youth work is based on.*

> *We talk about all sorts of methods for empowering young people and even how to consult with them. But actually, it's the relationship that youth workers make with young people that forms the basis for young people's development and empowerment. It's the relationship that drives the process forward. That one-to-one relationship outweighs everything else. It's the foundation on which everything else is built.*

> *If you ask young people what they value about the youth service they say the relationships with the staff. They always say that. They will give examples of being able to talk to workers about their family, school, relationships with other people and they may say: 'If I want to, they'll take me camping.' I don't think that really happens in their contact with other agencies. Not in any consistent way.*

However, whilst the relationship between the youth worker and young person has been a constant theme throughout the development of youth work, it is also the most elusive of all aspects:

> *The worker cannot quantify this relationship to those 'outside' and yet, because of this, the worker is left to attempt to assess youth work in terms of the demands of those 'outside'. The failure of youth work has been its own reluctance to argue for a validity of a view from the 'inside'. Indeed, most accounts of practice focus upon the activity, assessing the work with young people in terms of 'doing' rather than 'being'.*

> (Richardson, 1997: 91)

From activities to relationships

The reality, of course, is that most young people get involved in youth work because they are attracted by the activities or opportunities being offered. They do not necessarily, in the initial instance, come for the relationship about which they possibly have little knowledge. They come for the activities and the facilities and the cha⌐ce to do something. It does not even have to be that exciting or diffe   ⌐ometimes they simply need a warm and welcoming place to ⌐   ⌐riends.

A number of ye   there was a questionnaire of young people in the
rural villages. '   ⌐e report said was that young people had nothing to
do – which   ⌐olutely true. There is a real problem with access to
facilities. ⌐   ⌐ you ask young people around here what they want to
do they   ⌐ to the Dome in Doncaster', which is a place where they
can ta   ⌐ almost any activity you can think of. They don't say they
want   lucation' or a 'good listening ear from a youth worker'. After
the⌐   ⌐ to get involved in youth work they begin to recognise that
the⌐   ⌐omething to be gained from engaging in a relationship with the
youth worker which actually offers them more than they thought, because
they thought they were just going to get to go canoeing or climbing or
whatever. Here is something else that they didn't know about and were
therefore unable to anticipate. So two things happen. Firstly, they recognise
the relationship, and secondly, they come to value it.

It was a summer's day and these two old gentlemen started walking
towards us. At first, we thought it was someone's father but when he (the
worker) came up he had these bright yellow A5 leaflets and he introduced
himself and started telling us about some new project that was starting up
and invited us to the youth project to have a chat. We were a bit
apprehensive because you only really trust your own age group. Anybody
older is basically outside it. So we started cracking a few jokes to break the
ice and he started telling us what they were planning to do. And it seemed
like it was basically giving us some power to do things for ourselves like
residentials and activities and so on. So we went along. But in all honesty
it was basically for what we could get out of it for ourselves. That's what
it came down to. But from there on it developed into a relationship – with
trust.

When it first started off we just thought well if they want to do this for us
that's fair enough. We weren't doing anything apart from playing football
in the park and going down the arcade. So we thought great. Free
residentials, activities, things we'd never had the opportunity to do before.
But then most of us became aware that there was more to it than met the
eye. It was about social development, acquiring new skills for yourself
rather than just gallivanting off to whatever residential and doing activities.
It gave us the abilities and skills to organise activities for ourselves, which
meant that we would later be able to say we did this or organised that.
You had a certain idea about how to do things. Basically it made us look

inside ourselves and say, 'What am I doing here?' 'Where do I want to progress to in my life?' We also started looking at the neighbourhood and crime and thinking about what could be done about it. It was more or less a stepping stone for us to begin helping the community and in that way it encouraged more young people to join in the youth project.

Initially, young people may be attracted by the opportunity to take part in activities. They may decide to go along with things to see what they can get out of it for themselves – grasping the chance for a free week-end away or involvement in activities like canoeing or camping. It is only after this initial phase that they come to realise that there is more to youth work than they first thought. They acquire and develop new skills and abilities. They look inside themselves and ask, 'What am I doing here?' and 'Where do I want to progress to in my life?' They look at their neighbourhood and discover ways of helping the community.

Central to this experience is the voluntary relationship that is based on young people's agenda:

The voluntary relationship is crucial. Young people don't choose their parents, or choose to go to school. They choose to be here.

The relationship needs to be based on young people's agenda and not on the worker's agenda. So when they have an issue they go and talk to the youth worker and it's their issue. The youth worker is not trying to get them through the national curriculum.

Values

The relationship between youth worker and young person is also underpinned by a set of essential values identified by the workers and young people interviewed as:

- Accepting and valuing young people.
- Trust.
- Honesty.
- Respect.
- Reciprocity.

Obviously, these are overlapping. Acceptance, trust, honesty, respect and reciprocity are not separate entities. They combine together to create the broad foundation of the relationship within which the youth worker and young person explore and negotiate their own parameters. However, in taking a 'view from the inside' it is possible to identify and illustrate how youth work practice gives meaning to such concepts.

Accepting and valuing young people

If you are working with people you have to understand that a person is about emotions, feelings, values, things that happened to them years before you got there and the experiences they've had. Youth work is about protecting that, honouring it, valuing that person for who they are and recognising that we have inequalities in society that affect people's lives. Youth work is about acknowledging those differences and not pretending that we are all equal or just making sure that particular individuals can do certain things.

You need to be honest about where they are at and where you're coming from. It's about not being judgemental. That probably sounds like a cliché but particularly as an Asian woman worker I'm really conscious that if I'm working with young Asian women it's crucial that they very quickly realise that I'm not the sort of person who's going to judge them. Many of the things that happen in their lives are to do with the communities from which they come and to which I also belong, so it's very important that they actually see that I'd be non-judgemental and also maintain confidentiality about whatever it is they share with me. The important thing is for them to know that I will not judge them despite being a Hindu woman with the values and cultural norms that I come with.

I think youth work is about valuing people. The workers have really valued me, and what I believe in and who I am even though they don't always understand what I'm trying to do. They realise how important it is to me and so they're prepared to give me time and support.

Acceptance means accepting young people with all the emotions, feelings, values and history they come with. It means not judging young people whatever our cultural norms and values; and it means recognising how inequalities affect people's lives and seeking to challenge those inequalities as opposed to simply securing opportunities for particular individuals. Acceptance means valuing young people – giving them time and support.

Trust

To me, young people are no different from adults in the sense that they only share their hopes and fears with people they trust. Like adults, they are more likely to listen to and consider the views of somebody who they feel has their best interest at heart even if they are saying difficult things. That's very different from feeling that people are either trying to manipulate you or that they just don't care. So if workers are going to challenge young people about their behaviour or question the choices they make then that's only going to be accepted by young people if they feel there is some trust and respect in that relationship.

I'm quite honest with young people in terms of what I'm thinking about what they are saying and what they are doing. But if they listen to me it's because of the respect and trust that's built up between them and me not because I'm an adult in authority and therefore I'm right.

I am a volunteer leader now but I used to be a member at the centre and what I can remember I saw was trust and leaders who had patience and time who were bothered to want to help. With that kind of person you made a bond – someone that understands you and shows patience and time and trust and someone that just cares really. I think that's one of the most important things in youth work. You've got to really care about what you are doing because if you don't then there's no real point in doing what you're doing.

Young people, like other people, share their hopes and fears with people they trust. They are also prepared to consider the opinion of people they trust even if those opinions are difficult to take on board. But what makes a person trustworthy? The main message from those interviewed appears to be: 'You can trust people who care', people who take the time and show the patience and who are bothered enough to want to help.

The relationship between a youth worker and young person is therefore based on trust, honesty, respect, and the belief that the young person has the ability to change and grow.

Youth workers are trustworthy in the sense that you can tell them stuff and also if I needed someone they'd be there for me ... [the worker] is completely on my level – which is funny because before I got involved in youth work I didn't really think much of youth workers. I just thought they were prats. And then after a while I thought, 'God they earn so much respect and you really don't appreciate them'.

Honesty

I think youth workers should be completely honest and open with young people about who you are and what you are capable of. What you can or cannot do with them. There are times when young people think that you can do a lot more than you can. At those moments there's often a temptation to go along with it because you think if we can get them in we can get the numbers up and so on. But actually that's not what it's about.

The principles of trust and honesty are central to youth work. I need to trust young people as much as they need to trust me. But it's always me that has to be the first one to take that risk of putting trust in them. They have to feel that I trust them. I also have to be honest and not have hidden agendas with them. If I'm about to do something about which they should be consulted then I should consult them in an open and honest way. That's just showing respect, which is another important principle. Respecting them, their opinions, their talents and treating them as valued human beings.

The relationship between the youth worker and young person requires the worker to be honest and open about who they are, what they are capable of and what they have to offer. There is no hidden agenda in the youth work relationship. Workers consult with young people and 'put trust in them' – often being the first one to take that risk. Youth workers respect young people and their opinions, and treat them as valued human beings.

Respect

A youth worker does not have an automatic right to engage with a young person. I cannot assume that just because I am an adult that the young person wants to communicate with me. Therefore, the establishment of a relationship that is based on respect and trust is absolutely crucial. Besides, young people can always see through charades, through people who are patronising, people who are tokenistic, people who hide behind their authority.

It's about recognising that the situation a young person may be in is their situation. So we don't take a situation that the young person is in away from them, muck about with it and give it back to them and say, 'What do you think?' We keep them involved the whole time.

People need to feel connected to each other. Young people will only hear you if they have a level of respect for you and obviously if you are open and genuine but also if they can see that you do actually care about them. And if you don't actually care about them, young people pick that up very quickly. In fact some youth workers may even talk about a level of love for the young people that they work with – which means having positive regard for them. Viewing them as positive beings and being able to offer them support on their terms.

Respect in the relationship means recognising that youth workers do not have an automatic right to intervene in young people's lives or even to engage with them. Relationships are negotiated with trust and respect, and within an understanding that young people's lives, situations and issues belong to them. Respect means having a positive regard for young people, genuinely caring about them and being prepared to support them on *their* terms.

Reciprocity

Those interviewed also had a strong sense of the relationship as being two-way. That youth workers support young people knowing that young people also have skills, valid perspectives and expertise of their own. Young people also have something to offer, not only in practical ways:

> *If I go ice skating with young people they need to help me because I can't skate to save my life. But that's good because as youth workers we don't claim to be experts at everything. In fact, sometimes we need the young people's expertise which is good for them as much as for us.*

But also in terms of 'being there', their sensitivity and concern:

> *I try to be sensitive to young people's needs. I don't build their hopes and then disappear. The young people I'm working with know I'll be there when I'm needed so there's a much deeper kind of relationship between us. They have my home telephone number. I don't give it to all the young people. I choose who I give it to and it's those who I know won't abuse it. They'll use it when they need it and that's fine. Some also have my address at home and a few have visited me at home. Not necessarily because of any particular reason but just because they wanted to. They just felt like it. So they'll ring up and then come over. When they come to my house I make them welcome because I don't live in the area where I work and I acknowledge the effort they've made in travelling to see me – just because they wanted to see how I was. That's a reward that I find fascinating because it motivates me. You know we all work for money. If we didn't get money OK we might do a few hours of voluntary work but not full-time like this. You've got the mortgage to pay or whatever. But the financial side doesn't cheer me up. I think generally it doesn't cheer people up. It's the people you're working with. They are the ones who motivate you. So one of the things that I've always thought important in youth work is that you're not doing it for the money. You're doing it because you feel for young people. You have to feel their experience and what they're going through to actually do youth work. And you have to acknowledge it. Whether it's a positive or negative experience you have to feel for them and their needs in that situation. That's how they motivate you and you motivate them. It's done in partnership. Youth work is not a one-way process. It's not like I'm the youth worker and I'm expert at these issues and this is how it is. No. Young people have something to offer as well.*

> *Youth workers are like family. You know, someone who'll always be there. That's how I take them. You can let your guard down with them because they let theirs down with you. It's a two-way system. You give. They give. You respect them. They respect you.*

The youth worker as mentor

In their study of young people and mentoring, Philip and Hendry (1996) highlighted the qualities of 'helping relationships' as including honesty, respect, acceptance, (adult) interest in young people, trust (particularly in relation to confidentiality), empathy and elements of reciprocity, adults who are open to negotiation, and adults who are less authoritarian. These were the same qualities identified by interviewees in relation to youth workers relationships with young people.

In specifying these qualities Philip and Hendry asked young people to identify instances in which they had *felt* supported and challenged by individuals and/or groups. The result was the identification of five 'forms of mentoring': one-to-one; individual to group; friend to friend; peer group; and long term one-to-one.

But what distinguishes mentoring from other forms of 'helping relationships' and in particular, the relationship between a youth worker and young person?

- Firstly, the importance of long-term relationships where trust is assured and negotiation possible. Mentoring cannot, therefore, be conceived as a kind of 'one off' occasion. Mentoring takes place within the context of a relationship.
- Formality/informality represents the second significant feature of 'mentoring' relationships. Within the context of working with young people 'mentoring' schemes have been based on the assignment of mentors (Burke and Loewenstein, 1998) whereby mentoring is the expressed purpose of the relationship as opposed to 'mentoring' taking place within the context of an on-going relationship.
- This leads to the third significant feature – the question of purpose. In relation to working with young people, the 'mentoring' approach has been developed largely in the area of work with young people 'at risk', where the work is seen in terms of influencing the behaviour of young people for example in relation to offending, drug use or truancy. (NYA, 1997)

Such an approach contrasts with the experiences of the young people reported in the Philip and Hendry study for whom 'helping relationships' created space, time and support for their interests, needs and issues and finding solutions to their questions. So whilst mentoring can address an individual's skills or behaviour it works best when:

The need is the acquisition of wisdom. By wisdom we mean here the ability to relate what has been learned to a wide spectrum of situations, and to achieve insight and understanding into the issues discussed.

(Clutterbuck and Sweeney, 1997: 3)

Mentoring is, therefore, most effective when:

- It takes place within the context of an on-going relationship.
- It is informally initiated by the parties involved.

- It pursues the acquisition of wisdom.
- All parties make a personal commitment to the process.

Youth workers can, therefore, be seen as involved in the *activity* of mentoring, in the sense that they engage in informally initiated relationships with young people within which young people are supported and challenged to gain greater insight and understanding of themselves, their relationships and their world; and to which there is a deliberate commitment. This may take the form of the kind of one-to-one relationships, individual to group relationships or long-term one-to-one relationships which Philip and Hendry identify (1996).

However, youth workers are not formal 'mentors' in the sense that:

- They are not assigned. The relationship with the young person is voluntary and informal, and the nature and extent of guidance and challenge is (informally) negotiated with young people.
- Youth workers' work with young people focuses not on the priorities and concerns of others, but on the interests, needs and concerns of young people themselves.

He . . . [the youth worker] has had more experience than us. He's been there. He's seen it. And he's advising us. He's not telling us like our parents do. At first we didn't really take any notice. We just thought yeah, yeah, yeah. But over the years he's said things to us and even if we didn't take any notice at the time they've come back to haunt us. So then you think about it and you go, 'Oh yeah he was right'. And from that you say, 'All right let's see what he's got to say.'

I met [the worker] two years ago when I was 15 and trying to set up a self-help mental health project for young people who suffer from distress. At that time I think I was sort of having a breakdown but when I met [the worker] I was sort of coming through it. She was very open to new ideas and was very accepting. With her support I've now set up the group and won a Millennium Award so I've got funding for a year and I'm based at the Council House. But at the time I didn't really understand what her role was as a youth and community worker because I'd never even heard of youth and community workers before. So we had to work out what the relationship was and how she could best guide and advise me. That's not been easy because the workers have been very unsure and even frightened at times. But they thought here is a young person who is passionate about what she wants to do let's support her even if at times they didn't understand the issues involved.

The most important thing about the relationship is that it creates the environment for young people to explore their questions and answers, in a genuine and meaningful way. Conversations with young people begin with, 'How are you?' not 'what's your issue?

Yet, even these explanations do not adequately describe the relationship between a youth worker and young person. For in addition to the 'helping' qualities outlined above (acceptance, honesty, trust, respect, reciprocity), there is an added, more intangible quality that can, it seems, only be understood by way of comparison. In other words, by comparing the youth work relationship with some other relationship with which young people are familiar. For the young people interviewed that comparison is made in the form of a 'friend'. A youth worker is seen as being *like* a friend.

What is interesting is that while youth workers themselves tend to see this as problematic and are disinclined to describe the relationship as a kind of 'friendship', young people are often only too clear about the lines of demarcation. For them, youth workers are *like* 'friends' whilst at the same time not *being* 'friends'.

The youth worker as 'friend'

It's important that you get on with the youth workers because if you don't then there's not much point coming here. The relationship is like a friendship but it won't be such a strong friendship, just a mutual friendship where you respect them and they respect you. You can talk to them about anything really. Sometimes you may want to talk to a youth worker about things you are thinking about. Sometimes I may go to my friends. What makes youth workers different is that they are not controlling you. You come here because you want to, whereas with school you go there because you have to. So because you come here because you want to, it's a lot more friendly and you have a laugh.

Youth workers are sort of almost my friends. In fact, more than that. I can trust them with stuff I wouldn't tell my friends because I would be afraid that my friends might freak out and have a panic reaction. Like for example, when you first tell a friend that you are gay. If they've never met a gay person they might freak. But with youth workers you can tell them anything. They have some idea about how to deal with it. They can be supportive. Even if they don't agree with it, they're not judgemental. Unless it's about drugs and things like that, then they can be quite judgemental. They'll never march up to you and say, 'What you're doing is wrong. Stop it now.' But they have their own ways of telling you that maybe it isn't such a good idea.

A youth worker is like a friend because they see you grow up and they are always there. They know your family. They're there when you are in trouble. They know all about your life so they're sort of always in the background or in the foreground. It's like having a big sister or big auntie who you can tell things that you wouldn't tell anyone else. I know some people have sisters and aunties like that, but if you don't it's good to have a youth worker around. But youth workers are not your friends because you are not part of their social life. You are part of their work life.

Because youth work is mainly in the evening you can sometimes think it's social time and that you're friends with the youth workers. But you're not, so it can be frustrating. What you have to realise is that the youth worker's relationship with you is work. When I became a volunteer youth worker myself I understood it much more clearly. Like there are some of the girls in my group who I really like and would be friends with, but because their parents know me as the worker I can't go out with them on a personal level because I would always be responsible. Like if I went to a club or something then the parents would think, 'Why are you taking my daughter to a club? Is that part of your job description?' So you have to keep a clear boundary.

Youth workers are like 'friends' in the sense that there is mutual respect. Young people talk with youth workers about anything. Youth workers are not judgemental. They understand young people's issues and pressures. Young people choose to engage in the relationship. Youth workers are not controlling and young people can 'have a laugh' with them.

Youth workers are not 'friends' because young people are not a part of their social life. Young people sometimes tell workers things they would not tell their friends. Youth workers are more like family, an aunt or sister, who is always there. Youth workers have more experience and knowledge than peers. Youth workers maintain clear boundaries.

From the worker's point of view:

I am not their friend. I am there as a youth worker but I like to feel that the approach is friendly and that they can approach me and we can have a discussion and talk things through. In the process, I can and will challenge their comments, behaviour or attitudes and hopefully we can talk about that because they know I'm not coming with some kind of authoritarian attitude. The relationship is more informal. More flexible. Sometimes I'll get angry and sometimes they'll be angry with me. But at the end of the session it will be like, 'See you next week', because it's over and finished. Or it may not be. It may continue. But the important thing is that I get across to that young person that I still value them. I still support them and I still care about them as a person. I just don't care about some of their beliefs or attitudes and I make that difference perfectly clear.

Subscribing to the idea of the youth worker as 'friend' is problematic since the word carries connotations of socialising, which detract from the essential professional or work focus intended. As a result, many workers balk at the suggestion while young people seem much more able to draw a distinction between 'a friend' (i.e. peer) and someone who is 'like a friend' (a youth worker).

However, following Aristotle, it becomes possible to understand the concept of a friend as 'someone who likes and is liked by another person', given that liking is defined as:

> *Wanting for someone what one thinks good for his [sic] sake and not for one's own, and being inclined, so far as one can, to do such things for him . . . out of concern for him and not, or not merely, out of concern for oneself.*

(Cooper, 1980: 302)

But how do youth workers show such concern for young people? The young people and youth workers interviewed here identified four ways in which this concern is demonstrated. These were:

- Empathy.
- Listening to young people.
- Taking account of young people's views and ideas.
- Helping young people to 'see' themselves.

Empathy

> *One of our best part-time workers came here originally as a Prince's Trust Volunteer. Six years later, he is a qualified youth worker who may well get the other full-time post here. One of the key things about his relationships with the young people is that he comes from the immediate area. He started where lots of the young people are. He didn't fly in from middle class suburbia with all the qualifications and so on. He struggled to become qualified. And because he comes from this neighbourhood then it's easy for the young people to identify with him. He can empathise with their situation. He's been where they are. He can understand what they are going through as white working class kids living in this neighbourhood. They trust him and they want to talk with him about things that matter to them.*

> *The relationship is essentially empathetic. It is about seeing young people and young people feeling they have been seen. They have been recognised in some way, which is a kind of spiritual thing that's about self and a very fundamental recognition of one human by another in a very focused way. That's not an easy thing to do. And it's more difficult when you are busy. But I think it happens more often than not since the young people here are not simply seen as a mass to be serviced.*

Listening to young people

When I came here there was a leader who loved football and I got on really well with him and even though I wasn't the best behaved kid I felt I could trust him. He was understanding, and just listened and gave me attention. Teachers are doing their job. They don't care about your feelings. They don't listen. They just say, 'Oh you've got homework' or whatever. But here it's more like a community. It's nice.

The way youth workers connect with young people is crucial. That means giving a clear message that I am listening to you and you alone right now. Showing respect for young people's space – none of this head patting – metaphorically or physically – or come to me I'm a youth worker and you're my job.

Taking account of young people's views and ideas

The club is for young people with learning disabilities. When I first started there we didn't have members meetings. The workers decided what the young people wanted within the club programme and we decided how it was going to be run. I then started the members meetings and got a lot of hostility from some of the volunteers who said things like, 'Well, they'll never sit still for a start, never mind getting them to talk about what they want or how to build a programme'. So I had to get over that to start with and sometimes it was a case of even saying to some of the volunteers, 'I'd rather, if you're not going to take an active part in this and disrupt it by shuffling, moving, getting up, then I'd rather you just stayed out of the room'. So it took a long slow process to get the young people to actually say what they wanted and engage in a process of negotiation about what was possible. From that experience they started to realise that we were going to listen to them. So we were building up a relationship where they came to trust us more and more. They then started to tell us about what had gone on at school or what some of their personal fears were, how they were feeling, peer pressure, what some of their girlfriend or boyfriend issues were. It was a gradual process of building that relationship and responding to them with compassion, which made them more willing to discuss things about themselves and their lives.

The key thing is the relationship that youth workers have with young people. That relationship is about young people being able to open up and talk to us. They come in because they want to come in. They want to participate. They want to take part. If you look at schooling, social work – it's young people being told that they have to do it. But in youth work, it's about what young people want to do. It's about getting their ideas. Getting their views. And using their ideas and views to take them forward.

Helping young people to 'see' themselves

Before I met [the worker] I'd never had any contact with anyone else who I could talk to about my problems or experiences and who could actually help me to realise what I thought and make my own decisions. He doesn't tell us. He asks us and he gives his own viewpoint. Just his viewpoint. Rather than saying this is what you should do, he says this is what you could do. And that's a completely different way of saying something. Different from other adults. Also, he was on the same wavelength. He understood our language. Teachers were more formal. They used to speak more formally to us. So I felt more comfortable talking to [the worker] because I see him more as a friend whereas if I was talking to a teacher I wouldn't feel comfortable and there are things I wouldn't tell the teacher.

The relationship between youth worker and young person enables us to look below the superficial and explore opportunities for reflection. That's not to say that when you look at me, you see yourself, but that there is some kind of openness and willingness to be available on young people's terms. What you see is me reflecting you back to yourself. What you don't see is me, my ego, my problems, my issues, my worries, my experience of what you're going through. You will see yourself. That's the ideal. So this is more than just a mirror that reflects back and has no personality. It's about being there for the other person, as a role model that young people aspire to be whether it is because of wanting to be as thoughtful as the worker, as reflective, or sensitive or willing to listen.

The youth worker as role model

People model themselves on others through a process of observing others' actions and the consequences of others' actions, and adjusting their own behaviour. It is something we learn at an early age. Indeed, Bandura (1974) observed that this is the very process, which children use to learn language. Children observe the effects of different sequences of sound and words and imitate them. Some reproductions are verbatim. However, on many other occasions children re-construct their observations to create sentences they have never actually heard. In so doing, they move beyond mere imitation to grasp the ability to produce appropriate responses to new situations.

It is not just language that is learnt in this way. The process of imitation and re-construction accounts for many of the life skills that constitute our daily experience. For the most part such learning happens on a subconscious level. However, whilst this natural learning process has been developed into a highly structured learning technique (behaviour role modelling – Bandura, 1974) the informal nature of youth work means that 'role modelling' is likely

to remain somewhat ethereal. Nonetheless, youth workers are often described as role models for young people.

> Our project is about working with young people involved in or on the margins
> of the drug culture. But actually, the most important thing is not about giving
> them information or going in heavy about drugs. It's about making meaningful
> and constructive relationships with young people. That's the key. And in order
> to do that, you need consistency and continuity. You can't parachute into this
> kind of work.
>
> Offering a positive role model is crucial. That means being clear and explicit
> about your own values. Saying what you stand for. Drawing firm lines. And
> setting high standards for yourself and young people. Young people are not
> stupid. They know what is right and wrong and they believe in fairness. What
> they want to know is what you are about.
>
> Trust and credibility are not there for the asking. It's about being real and
> consistent. We have to do the right thing in the way we behave and interact
> and lead our lives. People see us everyday walking down the street or out
> shopping or whatever. We can't afford to be hypocritical because the success
> of this project rests on our integrity as people as much as our integrity as
> workers.
>
> We work from a Black perspective, which means five things to us. Firstly,
> recognising that we live in an inherently racist society and understanding race,
> racism and oppression as being socially constructed. We also think it is crucial
> to have an understanding of Black culture and history. Valuing education is
> important because knowledge is power, but actually, knowing how to use
> knowledge is more powerful. The Black perspective is also about doing
> something. Taking action and being positive about what you are going to do.
> Finally, it's about building on tradition and continuity and recognising the rich
> and lengthy tradition of youth work in this community which will continue long
> after the end of this particular project.

The idea of the youth worker as role model is therefore grounded in the
necessity for workers to practise what they preach. That is, the need to
establish the 'moral authority' that underpins their integrity as people and
gives credibility to their work as practitioners. It is not, therefore, so much a
case of imitation, but rather, establishing the value base or ethical framework
within which the youth work relationship operates. In other words, letting
young people know 'what you are about' and living true to it.

An inevitable consequence of the voluntary nature of the relationship
between young people and youth workers is that the latter, perhaps more
than other educators, rely on their moral authority to secure a constituency.
Securing and retaining such authority, often in trying circumstances, creates
an ever present tension within the work, for without resorting to
subterfuge they must seek to become the kind of people that young people

can trust, both intellectually and with regard to their character . . . steady, completely reliable and consistent.

(Jeffs and Smith, 1999b: 71)

However, the importance of the youth worker's 'moral authority' is actually about much more than merely 'securing a constituency' since the very intention of youth work is to engage young people in a process of examining and exploring values and morals. As one worker remarked:

We say that youth work is about informal and social education but I think it is actually about more than that. It's an education that is grounded in young people's active search to discover what they think and how they feel and where their values match up with their sense of who they are.

Engagement in such self-exploration cannot, therefore, be undertaken simply as a matter of developing the cognitive equipment needed for autonomous moral judgement. For youth work, like moral education, is not 'just or mostly a matter of moral reasoning, but a growth in our concern for what we are in our relationships with each other' (Kleinig, 1982: 252).

Therefore, the role model offered by youth workers not only establishes their 'moral authority', but also, and importantly:

- Creates the ethical framework for their relationships with young people; and
- Secures the basis for engagement in the process of moral philosophising which youth work necessarily involves.

Adults can seem like very scary figures sometimes but youth workers are usually down-to-earth characters. You can just sit down and chat with them about anything and everything for hours. It's really a lot of fun. Actually I'm baffled by the relationship. It's not like a social worker and a client relationship. It's more flexible. It's different. It's not like a parent and child. It's not like a teacher. Not like going to the doctors. It's not like anything. It's not like having a friend. It's like youth workers are none of these things but all of them rolled into one. So they need a kind of personality that's open to everything and the ability to talk to anybody and everybody. You need to be able to have a laugh with them. And if you think about [the worker] you can see that she genuinely cares about people.

Summary

Youth work is based on a voluntary relationship with young people that involves:

- Accepting and valuing young people.
- Trust.

- Honesty.
- Respect.
- Reciprocity.

These relationships involve 'conversations' through which the youth worker enables and supports young people to make sense of their lives, and learn from their experience.

In the process, the youth worker engages in the activity of mentoring whilst acting as a role model and 'friend' to young people in the sense of wanting for the young person what 'one thinks good for his or her sake and not for one's own'. This involves empathising with young people, listening to them, taking account of their views and ideas, and helping them to 'see' themselves.

The role model offered by youth workers establishes their 'moral authority' while:

- Creating the ethical framework for their relationships with young people; and
- Securing the basis for engagement in the process of moral philosophising that youth work necessarily involves.

Youth work process

Youth work is an educational activity and education, following Dewey, is a liberating experience that encourages reflective behaviour and promotes growth and health, developing the individual and supporting their participation in society (Dewey, 1961). Youth work is not, therefore, an activity for reforming young people or inculcating rigid patterns of socially required behaviour. Neither is it a static yardstick but rather a set of processes that must be re-assessed to meet the needs of different individuals, situations and circumstances.

As an educational activity youth work's intention is to liberate as opposed to domesticate young people in the sense that it offers them opportunities to:

> . . . *reflect on themselves, their responsibilities, and their role in the new cultural climate – indeed to reflect on the very power of reflection. The resulting development of this power [being] an increased capacity for choice.*

> (Freire, 1976: 16)

Once you've established some trust, a good way to begin is to give young people some responsibility. Running the café is a good example. It offers the chance for involvement and ownership. It's true that sometimes we've made a wrong judgement in giving out such responsibilities. Maybe the young person wasn't ready for it. Maybe they were so much in poverty that it was like putting it on a plate for them. But we're not talking about phenomenal amounts of money so there's always been the opportunity to discuss the whole issue of morals. And that has led on to conversations about what it means to have taken from your own community and then looking at where that young person is, why they are doing that and what their needs are.

Within the social education context a lot of the work is about enabling young people to explore and make choices whether it's about leaving home or all the other issues that come up. So what we try to do is to create a curriculum that gives them opportunities to explore moral issues. That is political sometimes. So in an agency like this, 'outing' is a regular discussion amongst young people. That enables us to tap into debates about the consequences of 'outing' – for example, loss of family, friends, job – and whether or not it is essential for people to be 'out and proud'.

We do a sort of 'problem page' session, which we normally recycle about once a term. During this, people are able to write down problems for the agony aunt to resolve. Generally what happens is the agony aunt, who will be one of the young people in the group, tries to promote debate. Through that process the young people will have an opportunity to explore rights and wrongs. Sometimes the staff put things in to provoke discussion because they know of an issue or something that's going on. For example, a while ago we realised that quite a few of the young people were working on the 'rent scene'. And although we'd talked about some of the issues and run some sessions on self-assertion it didn't work very effectively. But when we started using structured sessions with case studies and scenarios young people started to get more involved in the discussion and were more able to open up.

The youth work process is therefore a reflective exercise that enables young people to:

- Learn from their experience;
- Develop their capacity to think critically; and
- Engage in 'sense-making' as a process of continuous self-discovery and re-creation.

Learning from experience

The learning process in youth work involves reflection and deliberation. So learning is not envisaged simply as a process of 'inert ideas . . . [being] received into the mind without being utilised, or tested, or thrown into fresh combinations' (Alfred North Whitehead quoted in Freire, 1976: 36). Learning is seen as a dynamic process, which leads to action. In other words, to be meaningful, learning needs to be tested in reality. This process of learning is reflected in Kolb's (1984) experiential learning cycle which describes four stages:

1. *Concrete experience*: The young person's experience, whether arising from everyday life or some particular youth work intervention.

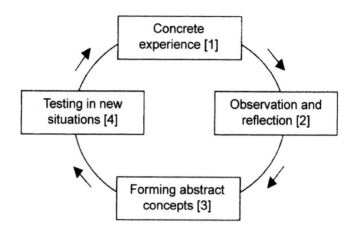

2. *Observation and reflection*: The opportunity for the young person to reflect on the experience, analysing not only what they think but also how they feel.

3. *Forming abstract concepts*: Through which the young person:
   – Examines their thoughts and feelings about this experience in relation to other situations and experiences;
   – Gathers information from other sources (e.g. other young people, the worker, other adults, books, newspapers, videos, etc.); and
   – Integrates these reflections and information into a generalised framework for decision-making and future action.

4. *Testing in new situations*: The 'testing' of the young person's new 'theory' in a real life situation – which, in turn, gives rise to new experiences that trigger a new learning cycle of reflection, understanding and testing in reality.

Of course, the young person's 'experience' may not necessarily be an event. It may be information they have received or ideas they have encountered. But whatever the nature of the 'experience', learning from it will necessarily involve the young person in reflecting, integrating their reflections with other information, and forming a new 'theory' that will guide their future thinking and action.

Critical thinking

Central to this process is the capacity to think critically. In other words, the capacity to:

- Identify and challenge assumptions.
- Recognise the importance of the social, political and historical contexts of events, assumptions, interpretations and behaviour.
- Imagine and explore alternatives.
- Question claims to universal truths or ultimate explanations (Brookfield, 1987).

Critical thinking therefore entails the ability to:

- Grasp the *meaning* of a statement.
- Avoid *ambiguity*.
- Spot *contradictions*.
- Judge what *follows*, what is *assumed*, and when a conclusion is *unwarranted*.
- Decide when a definition is *adequate*.
- Decide when an *observation, statement* or *authority* is reliable.
- Decide when a problem has been properly *identified* and adequately resolved (Ennis, 1962 cited in Fisher, 1991: 50).

This kind of reasoning is, of course, no easy task. It requires practise and is sharpened and perfected through disciplined discussion (Dewey, 1900, *The School and Society*, cited in Whalley, 1991) which re-affirms the central importance of conversation/dialogue within the youth work process. Indeed, according to Freire 'the mark of a successful educator is not skill in persuasion – which is but an insidious form of propaganda – but the ability to dialogue with educatees in a mode of reciprocity' (1976: xiii).

Conversation or 'dialogue'

'Dialogue' utilises people's own experiences in order to help them to develop their reflective behaviour. As such, dialogue enables and supports them to 'reflect on themselves, their responsibilities, and their contribution to society' (Freire, 1976).

> The relationship that young people have with youth workers here is informal. Most of the interaction takes place through conversation so the worker needs to be able to think very clearly about the conversations that go on with young people – what their role is or what kind of intervention they can make. To do that, you need to have enough knowledge and foresight about what is likely to happen next and a readiness to use conversations as opportunities to be in the role of an educator, albeit informal. That's what makes conversations meaningful.
>
> Meaningful conversations don't just happen. You have to create an environment for them to take place. An atmosphere that has warmth, fun, spontaneity. An environment that enables young people to broaden their

knowledge, understand the complexity of the issues they are involved in and express themselves in a clear, straight-forward and assertive way.

Jeffs and Smith (1999a) describe 'conversation' as involving:

- Concern – in being *with* our partners in conversation; engaging with them.
- Trust – taking what others say on faith.
- Respect – mutual regard.
- Appreciation – valuing the other's qualities.
- Affection – a feeling with and for our partners.
- Hope – faith in the inherent value of education.

By contrast, Green and Christian (1998) refer to 'accompanying' – a process which they liken to a pianist 'accompanying' a soloist. What is required, according to Green and Christian, is concentration and attention, and a striving to 'pick up the mood' of the soloist with sensitivity and awareness. 'Accompanying' means 'being alongside' young people, 'being there' (Green and Christian, 1998: 20). It is:

> *An empathetic conversation where one person supports another and enables them to explore the full range of emotions, thoughts and consequences of part of their life. Both the accompanied and accompanist have to listen to each other and are learning and growing from the conversation. However, the accompanist is giving the gift of a platform to the accompanied, who is then able to analyse, accept and make plans concerning their current situation.*

(Green and Christian, 1998: 23)

The qualities of 'accompanying' are identified as empathy, sympathy, tolerance, respect for the viewpoint of the accompanied, being grounded (or centred), personal space, life experience, understanding, wisdom, active listening, concentration and grace – awareness of the spirit moving in the lives of both the accompanied and accompanying person (Green and Christian, 1998: 28).

Conversations in context

Conversations are therefore the bedrock on which youth work is built. But conversations do not happen in a vacuum. Conversations have contexts. For example, conversations sometimes occur in the process of offering *personal support* to young people:

> *Before I met [the worker] I wasn't really into education. If I failed an exam I would just give up. But he's given me the sense to just carry on and work even harder at it. He's shown me a different kind of view if you like. And I've realised that if I get an education I've got a better chance of getting a*

job that I like instead of just working in a factory or something like that for the rest of my life. So if I hadn't met him I wouldn't be going to university. I would have probably found myself a job and started working on from there.

Youth workers also engage in conversations with young people in the process of helping them to explore their *options and choices*:

I view my role as ensuring that young people have an awareness that there are other options. For instance, if I'm talking to a young person who is doing his or her GCSEs and thinking about A levels, I might ask them, 'What has your careers advisor advised? What are you interested in? What do you dream about doing?' Their answer is very much located around going to work in this society, that's it. So I may explore with them other options such as developmental work in the Caribbean or another area of the developing world, volunteering for a Black organisation, VSO or simply not feeling pressured to make a fixed decision at this point, looking further than what the agenda of capitalism has to offer.

Sometimes youth workers utilise structured activities and situations to 'kick start' conversations that help young people to *think about their lives, their experiences and their values:*.

We ran a programme on decision making last year for the 16 + age group. We asked them things like how they made decisions about how their bedroom was going to look, how they decided whether to smoke or not – which is a always a big thing on residentials. How they decided what their signature was going to look like for the rest of their life. What sort of process did they go through? How did they want their signature to represent them? What did they want it to say about them? They were stunned. The main thing that came out of the session was us asking the questions because the response was 'My God no one has ever asked me such questions before and I've never thought about them.' And this is 16 to 19 year olds. After that it became possible to ask other questions like 'Why are you like you are? How come you are like yourself? How come you did this and not that? OK these are big philosophical questions for teenagers but the significant thing is they were so excited to be asked. During the course of the programme they became more reflective and more analytical. I think they responded differently to the programme because they suddenly got more excited about themselves. To explain themselves to someone else was really exciting for them, not as an interrogation but from the point of view of saying 'I've thought about it and I have this opinion', which was a revelation to them. And the fact that someone had asked them these questions and was prepared to engage in discussion meant that they come through expecting to be negotiated with.

We have a programme, developed jointly with the local adventure playground, that involves work with 10–14 year olds in four local primary schools. It's a structured series of weekly sessions based on ten key principles called 'Do The Right Thing'.

1. Treat others as you would like to be treated.
2. Listen and you will be heard.
3. Do not shout at just speak to others.
4. Positive attracts positive.
5. Achieving is believing and believing is achieving.
6. Each one, teach one.
7. Set your own standards, live by example.
8. Share and care for your own space.
9. Speak with your mouth, not with your fists.
10. Wake up to your faults and do something about it.

Young people are supported to think about these principles using structured exercises and discussion. Through this process they get to examine who influences them, who holds power, how to take responsibility for their own actions, how they would like to see their community and what positive change they can effect.

The drama group has been working on a play about alcohol. But something that kept coming up again and again was a load of stuff around domestic violence and relationships that the young people in the group have with their fathers in particular, but parents in general . . . So as workers we thought it important to recognise what was happening. When we went on the residential we said, 'OK we're not doing drama this weekend. This is about domestic violence and our relationships with our families' . . . So for example, the part-time worker ran a session on domestic violence. I ran a sort of debate about gender relationships between women and men – what that means for us in terms of our values, our cultural values, our personal values. So there are times when you have to create space to make those kinds of conversations overt. But before that can happen you have to be open to recognising that there is a need.

We often use structured exercises to get into conversations about values. For example, one of the exercises we use begins with a brainstorm of the qualities that people look for in friends. Then through discussion and mutual agreement, we get that list down to half a dozen of the most important qualities. Each young person then has to choose the two qualities they consider most important and buy them using monopoly money. This always produces some very interesting conversations about friendship, what people are looking for, what they are prepared to give, whether it's possible to find the perfect friend, or whether, in the interest *of having some friends, we actually compromise. So for instance, if an important quality in a friend is someone who never lets you down does that mean that you don't have many friends because people often do let you down.*

We use all sorts of activities to help young women think about and work out their values – like a problem page activity or something like that where you get the problem and each group has to write their answer. We use activities like that to help us think about what's right, while recognising that there's not necessarily one right answer. So for example, there may be a value about respecting other people but there's not necessarily a right way of handling a situation. What's important is that young women get the chance to talk through the different ways you might handle a situation while recognising the important principles involved.

Conversations involve discussion of the whole range of *issues* important in young people's lives. For example, issues about the environment:

Through being involved with the youth club I've been to so many places and done so many things and met so many people that I just wouldn't have. I think my development has been one third me, one third just maturing through the passing of time and one third ... (the worker) because I wouldn't have done what I've done and thought about what I've thought about if it wasn't for her. Like when we were younger we used to go to this environmental group and it wasn't that much fun it was just fun because it was summer and a nice centre and a few nice people there. But eventually, I just never throw litter anymore. Because of that one little group that I went to. I hate throwing litter. It's things like that that you pick up. Also, I know people from all over the world because of the youth exchanges we've been on. And you can just see that slowly but surely things are changing. You don't always realise that when you are younger you just want something to happen now. But things are changing. I've also become much more confident because when I was younger she was the only Asian woman youth worker I knew and I thought that was wonderful because she was like a role model so I sort of do similar things like not judging people and just giving them a chance.

Issues about health:

What I think we're trying to do is to help young people develop the skills to make decisions and choices. So that's what all the information and resources I've developed for youth workers is about really. It's about saying to them 'Look how are young people going to make choices if they don't have the skills and ability to make those decisions'. Sure all the resources we've developed have been about health topics but the issue is about the approach. They're not just about information. They're about helping young people to develop the skills to make those decisions. I think that youth workers are particularly well placed to do this work with young people because of the voluntary nature of youth work. Young people come to youth organisations in their own time. They don't have to come. Whereas with parents I think you always aspire for your child to be growing up in a certain way. Schools, although they talk quite a lot about empowering young people, are not really able to do it because the system doesn't allow you to – as much as you might want to. Certainly there may be exceptions because there are some good teachers who are able to do this kind of work but it's very difficult. So what I come back to is the voluntary relationship and the youth worker's acceptance of that young person as a person because they are used to working with different young people with various backgrounds, various needs, conflicts and problems.

Issues concerning global inequalities:

I would use the accoutrements that young people value as a tool to create change. For example, they value fashion and clothes. So we would look at fashion. I might use a video for instance about trainers. How trainers are made. How much the people in Taiwan or wherever they make the trainers get paid a week. How much does it actually cost to make the trainers. And why are they selling you a trainer for £100 when it only costs £20 or £10 or £5 to make? What do you think that's about? In essence, get them to think about this concept that they have about instant gratification. 'How can something that is material make you feel good?' It's a sophisticated argument that you have to keep at a level they understand. Somehow you have to challenge them as to where they are. Young people may resist because in some ways they're quite happy where they are. But as a youth worker you know that the impact doesn't necessarily come today or tomorrow. The impact comes six, seven years down the road when you meet a young person who at one time was a regular at your unit and in your interaction with them you can see the growth and development and the measure of the challenges that they had.

Issues around difference and commonality:

There's too much going on in the world that's about harming each other. If you look at ethnic cleansing, the wars that go on, the way that young people get treated. All those things. I think if you can make a connection, make someone think about someone else and go beyond their own well being then you've done something useful. So that's why I've got a real bee in my bonnet about trying to make connections between people who are different. Particularly culturally or ethnically or racially or religiously different from each other. There's a time bomb out there that will explode sooner *or later and actually it's already exploding around us but we are not awake to it. We're nicely cosily living in our nice little homes with our nice little jobs. We get young people into the youth project but we are creating all of these islands of work with different groups of young people with very little connection between them. What I think we need is more opportunities for young people to find out about each other in terms of the differences that exist between them, for example as Sikh or Muslim, but also be able to explore the common ground between them which may be from the ethics or value base that each of us come from. I think it's about us, as workers, being able to articulate that and being able to enable young people to reflect upon it. So yes, you can celebrate the differences but you also need to look at what it is we have in common.*

Sense-making

Youth workers work within a diversity of issues and contexts, yet their conversations with young people are essentially about one thing – the development of young people's ability to 'make sense' of themselves, their experiences and their world. And this is achieved through providing opportunities that enable conscious and deliberate examinations of experiences and meanings.

The personal narrative is a special kind of story that every one of us constructs to bring together the different parts of ourselves into a purposeful and convincing whole. Like all narratives, the personal narrative has a beginning, middle and end, and is defined according to the development of plot and character. A personal narrative represents one of the ways in which we narratively structure and configure life insofar as it is an 'act of imagination that is a patterned integration of our remembered past, perceived present and anticipated future . . . we do not 'discover' ourselves in narrative, rather, we make or create ourselves through narrative . . . we create a narrative so that 'our lives, and the lives of others will make sense'.

(McAdams, 1993: 92).

Through narrative we define who we are, who we were and who we may become in the future. Hence to make meaning in life is to create 'dynamic narratives that render sensible and coherent the seeming chaos of human existence'.

(McAdams, 1993: 166 quoted in Crossley, 2000: 67)

But this is no simple matter.

When people talk about their lives, people lie sometimes, forget a lot, exaggerate, become confused and get things wrong. Yet they are revealing truths. These truths don't reveal the past 'as it actually was', aspiring to some standard of objectivity. They give us instead the truths of our experiences ... Unlike the Truth of the scientific ideal, the truths of personal narratives are neither open to proof nor self-evident. We come to understand them only through interpretation, paying careful attention to the contexts that shape their creation and to the world views that inform them.

(Personal Narratives Group quoted in Riessman, 1993: 22)

People's narratives are therefore not 'true' accounts of their experiences but accounts of the 'sense' they have made of their experience. In other words, the interpretations they have woven based on their emotional responses, existing understandings and the social, political and historical contexts within which those understandings and assumptions are located.

However, sense-making is not merely a case of constructing reality – i.e. re-interpreting the past to conform to the present, or alternatively, interpreting the present so as to create a continuous relationship with the past (Berger and Luckman, 1967). Sense-making is a discrete process, which has, according to Weick (1995) seven distinct characteristics that distinguish it from other explanatory processes such as understanding and interpretation:

According to Weick the process of 'sense-making' is:

1. Grounded in identity construction – since the question of 'who I am' is answered through discovery of 'how and what I think'.
2. Retrospective – in order to learn what I think I look back over what I have said and done in the past.
3. Enactment – by saying and doing things I create new situations that can be inspected for clues about what and how I think; and who I am.
4. Social – what I say, single out (events, actions, thoughts) and conclude are the result of who socialised me, how I was socialised and the 'audience' I anticipate will scrutinise my conclusions.
5. On-going – my talking is spread across time, competes for attention with other on-going projects and is reflected on after it is finished.
6. Focused on and by extracted cues – I single out and embellish a small portion of events, actions and thoughts because I identify them as salient within the context and my personal dispositions.
7. Driven by plausibility rather than accuracy – sense-making is not about creating accurate accounts but rather accounts which are coherent and credible.

Therefore sense-making is:

Something that preserves plausibility and coherence, something that is reasonable and memorable, something that embodies past experience and expectations, something that resonates with other people, something that can be constructed retrospectively but also can be used prospectively, something that captures both feelings and thought, something that allows for embellishment to fit current oddities, something that is fun to construct. In short, what is necessary in sensemaking is a good story.

(Weick, 1995: 60)

But personal stories are not merely a way of telling someone (including oneself) about one's life. Personal stories are actually the means by which identities may be fashioned (Rosenwald and Ochberg quoted in Riessman, 1993: 2). Therefore, a person's identity is to be found in their capacity to 'keep a particular narrative going' (Giddens, 1991: 54), since:

Self-identity ... is not something that is just given, as a result of the continuities of the individual's action-system, but something that has to be routinely created and sustained in the reflexive activities of the individual.

(Giddens, 1991: 52)

Sense-making is therefore a process of self-actualisation the moral thread of which is authenticity, that is being true to oneself – a process that requires being able to find oneself as well as being able to disentangle the true self from the false self (Giddens, 1991: 79).

The role of the youth worker can, therefore, be seen as engaging with young people in a process of moral philosophising that enables them to develop a consistent set of values that:

- Inform their identity; and
- Support their development as authentic human beings.

In the process, 'sense-making' becomes an integrated activity since people do not usually stop to make sense, they do it as they are going along – reflecting critically on their experience and creating new meanings for their lives (Wallemacq and Sims, 1998).

Summary

This chapter examines youth work practice in terms of:

- The nature of the youth work relationship within which young people are accepted and valued and which are based on honesty, trust, respect and reciprocity;
- The function of the youth work process in supporting young people to learn from their experience; and
- The role of the youth worker in enabling young people to make sense of themselves, their lives and their world.

Integral to this is **conversation**, since it is through narrative that 'people organise their experience in, knowledge about, and transactions with the social world' (Bruner quoted in Cortazzi, 1993:1).

Chapter 4

Art

As we have already discussed youth work engages young people in a process of moral philosophising, which enables and supports them to develop their sense of identity and cultivate themselves as authentic human beings.

In practice this involves a voluntary relationship with young people established within a framework of acceptance and valuing young people, honesty, trust, respect and reciprocity. Through reflective conversations youth workers support young people to learn from their experience and make sense of themselves, their lives and their world.

The 'art of youth work' is the ability to make and sustain such relationships with young people and provide the environment and opportunities for them to engage in moral philosophising. In order to successfully undertake such work youth workers need to be skilled, not only in the areas of group work and facilitating learning from experience, but also in skills such as effective communication and boundary setting; and qualities such as honesty, friendliness, humour and patience.

Central to this is youth workers' values since values underpin youth work, impact on it and create the foundation for young people's moral reflections. In order to become effective practitioners youth workers therefore need to commit themselves to continuous reflective practice so as to constantly revisit, review and renew their values and underlying ethical framework.

Skills and values

Youth workers need highly developed and effective interpersonal skills in order to establish and build positive relationships with young people. They also need group work facilitation skills and an understanding of group dynamics; an ability to critically appraise and evaluate practice; an understanding of how she or he uses him or herself in practice; knowledge of the context within which one is working – social, political, economic; an ability to act as an advocate when necessary but also knowing when to enable young people to speak for themselves. Youth workers need to be confident and comfortable about their own identity and how that has shaped their own values and beliefs. He or she needs to be able to be articulate and express what these are.

Youth workers need to be able to engage with other professionals from different fields and with parents. We need to see young people as a part of their community and work so that the community sees them as stakeholders in it.

We also need not to be 'experts'. It can be very reassuring to a young person to hear an adult say 'I don't know' or 'I never thought of that' or 'I don't understand' as often young people are afraid to say these things. They see it as a sign of weakness. We also need to know our own limitations and be able to say 'I'm sorry' or 'I was wrong' or 'I shouldn't have done that'. We need to be accountable to young people for our actions as well as to those who manage and fund us.

This might seem obvious but youth workers need to like young people. Need to get a kick out of working with them. Need to enjoy their energy, laughter, spontaneity and tendency to be politically incorrect. It can be very refreshing.

Effective youth work practice also requires that workers earn the trust and respect of the communities in which they work:

There is partly an assumption of trust in the community – trusting the worker to be non-judgemental, unconditional positive regard for them as human beings.

Last year I wanted to go to Pakistan with the youth project and I told my parents about it and they just smiled at me and said, 'OK son you're going to Pakistan.' But the more into it I got then my parents said, 'Oh you can't go because who is going to take care of you' and things like that. I spoke to [the worker] and he spoke to my parents and because he spoke to them about the project and they knew he was older and wiser and he'd been there before they gave me the chance to go with him because they gave him that responsibility to take care of me.

Skills

The youth workers and young people interviewed in the process of this work identified the need for youth workers to have good communication skills and the ability to listen and empathise. Youth workers were also seen as needing to be honest, friendly, humorous, observant, patient and able to set boundaries. Youth workers also need to have commitment and faith in themselves and those around them; and be able to support young people through their learning cycle.

However, such skills are not practised in a vacuum since youth work is underpinned by youth workers' understanding of young people's lives.

Young people are the experts of their own world. Our responsibility is not to know it, but to try to understand a little of it – just as much as they want to offer. That certainly helps me to be mindful about how I work with them so that I'm not going to offend them unknowingly or make them feel uncomfortable or open a door and quickly close it again. Then it's about creating the situations for them to want to take the plunge if you like – to make some choices. And then being there to support and help them think about what they learned or how they could have dealt with the situation in a different way or how could they have made it more beneficial or successful – without causing them to feel like they're rubbish or they've made a big mistake.

Young people often say that adults don't understand. That we've forgotten. I think that's often true. Sure we can talk about the character-istics of adolescence but we don't always remember what it actually felt like and the impact those changes have on you as a young person. So I think the job is about listening and hearing. It's about seeing things with a 16 year-old pair of eyes not using the hindsight that I have at 30-something and saying, 'Well you know this will happen'. It's actually about trying to understand how they see it, how big it is to them and what's important about it to them. Not what's important to us. OK, it might not be big in two weeks' time but in that moment it is big and needs to be afforded the same significance we attach to the things we identify as important. The main thing is to affirm young people and their experience – what they are saying and what they are feeling. Who feels it, knows it.

The relationship and work is also, in some instances, enhanced by some particular characteristic of the worker:

For some people it helps that [the worker] is a Muslim. They would feel more comfortable talking to him knowing that he is a Muslim as well. I feel more comfortable talking to him because we are both Pakistani. It's just one of those things really. It just helps you to build up trust knowing that he's from the same religion.

I'm not an overtly religious person. I fast and attend Friday prayer but I wouldn't call myself a religious person because you're meant to pray five times a day and that's what I class as religious. The fact that [the worker] is a Muslim is completely irrelevant to me. The only time it has helped me is when we've had a talk on religion and he has been there and been able to answer my questions. But that's because he just happened to be there and he's more educated than I am. The thing is though that [the worker] can speak Punjabi and the first time he came up to me and spoke to me in Punjabi I was really taken aback. Then he asked me what village I was from. And I thought, 'How do you know these things?' It broke down some barriers and kind of made the whole relationship relaxed and more personal. The Punjabi language is my identity. Most of my friends can't speak Punjabi they speak a different dialect. So [the worker] speaking Punjabi makes me feel closer to him because he knows where I was from.

If [the worker] was a white worker I think there'd be a lot more mistrust. I don't know why. But I do think it would probably take more time to actually trust him because you'd have to work much harder on the relationship and you'd be thinking in your head all the time, 'Is he thinking I'm a bad person because I talk like this?' In your head you'd probably be picking out the little things and feeling uneasy and wondering, 'does he understand the culture? Does he understand what goes on at home?' And thinking he can't really. Unless you've lived it, you can't really know what's going on.

However, according to interviewees, being an effective youth worker is not simply about accumulating a comprehensive set of skills (although skills are important). Neither is it about the youth worker's personal characteristics (although this too is important). In the end, good youth work practice rests on the youth worker's values.

Values

It's about attitude. Accepting where young people are coming from. Not putting them down but gaining their trust and being able to explore with them. There's a difference between a young person saying something and you just telling them they shouldn't have said it; and letting them say it and working out what's the belief underneath it. It's about adults who accept and value young people and who don't see themselves as somehow above them. That's where you have to be to start as a youth worker. Being non-judgemental is very important. So if my values are different from a young woman's parents' values then I need to explain to her what I believe without judging her parents as wrong because in the end she has to choose. You can't be in the position of turning her against her family. She has to grow into someone different if she chooses. The role of the worker is to open up the possibility that there is another point of view.

Youth workers' values are important because they impact directly on the work:

As a youth worker you can't impinge your own values on young people. I come from a background that is very middle class and I work with young people that are at the lower socio-economic class in terms of their parents being unemployed and things like that. It would be very easy for me to say, 'Well you should be doing this or you should be doing that'. So I think youth workers need to make sure that they look at their own values, and particularly in terms of how their values affect the way they are working with young people and dealing with the particular issues they are working with.

The youth worker needs to be constantly aware of her or his own prejudices and bias when it comes to combating structural inequalities. In terms of Northern Ireland, you have to be aware that very few venues are perceived as 'neutral' and often young people do not feel safe travelling outside of their own areas. Even a simple thing like wearing a particular football shirt can be divisive, provocative and dangerous. Words and phrases can also be insulting and derogatory without the young person knowing this to the full extent. There is also a lot of distrust and a lack of knowledge about the facts of history. In Northern Ireland there are always two versions of every story and very few workers who know both – including me.

Youth workers' values are also important because they underpin practice and create the foundation for young people's moral reflections:

My values are central to the way I work with young people. I feel quite privileged coming from a spiritual base that is a Hindu base because I don't feel any need to evangelise. But there are things about my values which come from my spirituality that I think are also common to people in general – like not wanting to hurt other people, taking on board that your actions may have an impact on other people so you have to think about what it is you are doing. You could even go back to the Ten Commandments I suppose if you wanted to say, 'Don't kill, don't steal', and the basic differentiation between good and evil that is there in everybody's faith. Issues around honesty for example – doing unto others as you wish to be treated yourself which is one of those core themes that I think is universal but we don't talk about anymore. I think another important value is about taking the time to reflect on your life. Wanting to give other people a chance is another. All of these are part and parcel of the values I hold and consider crucial in my relationships with young people.

My search for understanding is a part of my faith. It gives me something to fall back on. It means I don't have to have all the answers. What I do have is a way of working through my questions and an ethical framework that helps me to make sense of the issues around me. As a youth worker, my faith helps me to support young people to find a path that's clear for them. I help them to make sense of the spiritual teachings they have received and consider how to relate these to their everyday life – particularly when they need to come through a difficult time.

My values affect my relationships with young people through them realising that: 1. I don't mean them any harm; 2. I do have their interest at heart;

3. *That my contact with them is borne out of honesty, respect, caring – all of which come from a deeper commitment to people in general but to them in particular because that's the area I'm working in. I think if they know that, and most of them do, then the relationship can operate at a greater depth. So that would mean that they would be able to openly ask questions about doubts they might have about their lives. There may be experiences in their lives that are pivotal and may be harmful or hurtful to them that perhaps they can share with me in confidence. Actually, many of the young people I work with do come with some very damaging things that have happened to them. They feel able to talk about these because they sense that the relationship with me operates at a different level from the relationships they may have with other adults.*

Ethical practice

In the process of such practice, youth workers encounter a range of ethical issues, problems and dilemmas. Some of these may arise because they are *working* (which involves specific duties and responsibilities) with *young* people (who may have fewer rights and may be regarded as vulnerable in some way) (Banks, 1997). Others may concern issues of confidentiality or dilemmas about the need to safeguard the welfare of different individuals and groups – e.g. the young person, the community, or the agency (Morgan and Banks, 1999).

As a youth worker working with young people with disabilities it's very difficult to know where the balance is between what is practical and what, in an ideal world, should actually be happening. I sometimes face terrible dilemmas of wondering how much I should be talking with young people about contraceptives or relationships for example. Not just about the physical aspects but in terms of the feelings and what relationships actually mean to them. I ask myself, 'When do they have the space to do that?' And the truth is they often don't. There is so much anxiety and pressure from parents, guardians who have an influential role and others that there's never any time or space or privacy for them to discover what relationships mean to them. So whilst I might want to support young people to think about those things, I know some parents would not find that acceptable.

It is very difficult to work with young people in Northern Ireland around the issue of identity. And while political education and cross community work has been on the youth service curriculum since 1987, I think it's very difficult to be effective if nothing happens with adults in the community while young people are engaged in their programme. But it's not only that young people are seen to be divorced from their community, it's also that so many parents are actually openly opposed to cross community work.

This means that youth workers need to be:

- Clear about the 'code of ethics' that guides their practice (for example The National Youth Agency's *Ethical Conduct in Youth Work*, NYA, 2001).
- Committed to reflecting on their practice and clarifying their values.

A commitment to reflecting on your own practice is crucial. You need to be able to acknowledge your mistakes and accept criticism. So if a young person says 'You were wrong to do that to me', then you have to take it on board and come clean.

Youth workers have to be open to their own learning. They need a commitment to training and a commitment to looking at their own practice and really reflecting on the way they work with young people. That's really important to me. It matters because it's people's lives you're working with and so getting it right or being on the right track to working positively with them is very important. I learn so much from them as well and I love that.

Reflective practice

Therefore, youth workers need, as a matter of routine, to constantly revisit, reflect on and renew their values. Such a commitment to reflective practice requires practitioners to:

- Question 'taken-for-granted' assumptions about the definition of problems and categorisation of need.
- Recognise the ways in which ideas, thoughts, understandings and opinions are shaped historically, economically, politically and socially through social structures and processes.
- Make the implicit explicit.
- Raise the profile of value positions and working with the problematics they generate.
- Locate practice in its agency contexts so that service delivery issues are not addressed as routine constraints.
- Build reflection, involvement and evaluation into every stage of the practice process. (Everitt, Hardiker, Littlewood and Mullender, 1992: 134)

However, the need for youth workers' clarity and commitment in relation to their values is not simply because of the necessity to develop critical reflective practice or resolve ethical dilemmas. The need arises from the necessity for youth workers to be, themselves, well versed in the reflective and deliberative processes through which they seek to support young people.

Indeed, the idea that those involved in social education should engage in philosophical reflection is not new. Pring (1984) suggested that a part of the 'professional job of those who introduce personal and social education into the curriculum' should include:

. . . a careful, philosophical reflection upon what it means to be a person, how development as a person is inextricably linked with a form of social life, and where moral values and ideas are presupposed in both.

(1984: 167)

Earlier, Davies and Gibson had emphasised the need for the worker to 'understand what sort of person he himself is, what his needs are and what his beliefs and values are' (1967: 186).

And earlier still, the McNair Committee had commented that:

A well-informed philosophy of life, which may or may not be professedly religious, is most necessary to the youth leader; indeed, it is not easy to conceive of a successful youth leader without it.

(HMSO, 1944: 101)

However, philosophy is not enough since a 'well-informed philosophy of life' can only have integrity if it informs action. That is to say, it is not enough to know what is 'right', one must also seek to act 'rightly'. For, as Aristotle noted:

The object of our enquiry is not to know the nature of virtue but become ourselves virtuous . . . it is necessary therefore to consider the right way of performing actions, for it is actions as we have said that determine the character of the resulting moral states.

(Aristotle, trans., 1987: 44)

Therefore, according to Aristotle, a person acquires virtue by doing virtuous acts:

It is by doing just acts that we become just, by doing temperate acts that we become temperate, by doing courageous acts that we become courageous.

(Aristotle, trans., 1987: 43)

The challenge for youth work training and professional development is how to support workers to develop their 'philosophy' in terms of a clear set of values; and the 'habit' of acting ethically – that is a disposition towards finding right action in particular circumstances and acting from right motive. For the power and influence of the youth worker lies not simply in their relationships with young people but crucially in the constant weighing of ethical decisions and values which constitutes their daily practice.

Philosophy and 'the habit'

The problem is that most people only have the vaguest idea of what it might be to lead an ethical life. They understand ethics as a system of rules forbidding us to do things. They do not grasp it as a basis for thinking about how we are to live. They live largely self interested lives, not because they are born selfish, but because the alternatives seem awkward, embarrassing, or just plain pointless. They cannot see any way of making an impact on the world, and if they could, why should they bother? Short of undergoing a religious conversion, they see nothing to live for except the pursuit of their own material self-interest. But the possibility of living an ethical life provides us with a way out of this impasse.

(Singer, 1997: vi)

In this context, the issue is less a question of youth workers leading ethical lives and more a concern with youth workers developing ethical practice – assuming, indeed, that such things can be so separated.

The point here is that, in an occupation like youth work, reflection and discussions about principles and values are not merely intellectual exercises since there is an intention that 'discussion' should lead to both individual and collective action. Therefore, understanding participation, for example, involves not only an intellectual understanding but also acting in ways that enable young people to participate, which, in turn, requires an understanding of the concept of participation. The process is somewhat circular but represents what Plato called 'philosophy' (an understanding of virtue) and 'habit' (a disposition towards acting virtuously) which he considered to be the two essential components of an ethical education.

The training and development of youth workers therefore needs to include, at its very core, an ethical education that seeks to:

- Extend workers' personal and professional philosophy.
- Encourage their 'intelligent disposition' towards acting virtuously – i.e. exercising practical reason and judgement within a 'coherent system of precepts' or ethical framework.

This is not such a straight-forward matter as being guided by a 'code of ethics' or having the capacity to recognise and resolve ethical problems and dilemmas. For central to youth work is the ability to interpret and give meaning to the concepts and values involved: for example participation, empowerment, respect and social justice.

In terms of their training, youth workers need a clear understanding of their role and the fact that youth work is a job. They need to reflect on practice and they need to learn how to set boundaries and hold them. There are also some skills like group work, facilitation skills and dealing with conflict, which are important. But something that is in some ways more important is the opportunity to engage in a positive personal development experience. The sort of experience that encourages you to explore your views, hopes, fears, aspirations, values, what being you means to you and how your experiences have shaped your values and your life. Really it's about the development of them as people. It's almost like going through the same sort of experience they will be engaging in with young people. In 'Starting From Strengths' there was a recognition that in the first six months, part-time staff were often having a personal development experience themselves rather than working with the young people. That was right in the sense that they needed the time and attention to reflect and develop as practitioners. But sometimes when people leave college courses they haven't themselves had that sort of experience. If they are going to help young people to understand themselves and their lives then I really do think that they need to have experienced it themselves.

But how can youth workers be encouraged and supported to explore their 'views, hopes, fears, aspirations, values and experiences' in relation, not only to themselves as people, but in terms of their role as youth workers?

For surely it was Dewey who, in modern times, foresaw that education had to be redefined as the fostering of thinking rather than the transmission of knowledge; that there could be no difference in the method by which teachers were taught and the methods by which they would be expected to teach; that the logic of a discipline must not be confused with the sequence of discoveries that would constitute its understanding; that student reflection is best stimulated by living experience, rather than by formally organised, desiccated text; that reasoning is sharpened and perfected by disciplined discussion as by nothing else and that reasoning skills are essential for successful reading and writing; and that the alternative to indoctrinating students with values is to help them to reflect effectively on the values that are constantly being urged on them.

(Lipman, 1988 quoted in Whalley, 1991: 69)

Lipman's reference to teachers is no less relevant to youth workers in the sense that there should be no difference in the method by which youth workers are trained and the methods by which they are expected to work with young people. Therefore, youth workers need to be able to think. Their reflection is best stimulated by living experience. Their reasoning should be sharpened and perfected by disciplined discussion. And they should be helped to reflect effectively on the values that are constantly being urged on them and those which the practice of youth work demands.

Such 'disciplined discussion' could be envisaged as containing three essential components:

1. Serious discussion about values including getting people to see what it is like to live according to various value judgements.
2. Promotion of sensitivity to others and the consequences of one's actions.
3. Discussion of moral rules and principles – e.g. respect for persons.
   (Kupperman, 1983)

In addition, such discussion should, following Dewey, focus on workers' own personal and work experiences and help them to reflect effectively on the values that inform and underpin their lives and their work as youth workers. This would require a structured supervision process for both part-time and full-time workers based on learning from experience and providing opportunities for them to:

- Develop their skills in critical thinking.
- Engage in disciplined discussion about values and moral principles.
- Develop the practise of virtue through action, reflection and learning.

Indeed, the need for such an approach lies within the very practice of youth work itself, insofar as youth workers need to establish the 'moral authority' of those who 'practise what they preach'. (Jeffs and Smith, 1999a)

> *I suppose in the end what we are trying to do is to get young people to control themselves through making the right choices. Not just in terms of what we think are the right choices but the choices that are genuinely in their interest in terms of furthering their well-being. The best way to do that is that we also control ourselves, but you cannot do that unless you have analysed yourself. I think that's one of the most important things you should get from a training situation.*

Youth workers also need some basis for resolving the various ethical issues, problems and dilemmas encountered in their work (Banks, 1999).

> *One of the problems is knowing what right you've really got to be talking about morals with young people. So for instance how can you talk with them about not taking drugs and then go off for a drink at the end of the evening with the other workers. I know that alcohol can be as harmful as any of these other drugs. Therefore, who am I to say, 'I'd rather you didn't do that' when I know that if that young man said to me, 'I'd rather you didn't go to the pub', I wouldn't take any notice of him.*

Attention to values is necessary because youth work demands it.

> *We have created a monster in Wales and the monster in Wales is the curriculum statement. Because if you now go around and talk to workers about what they are doing they say, 'We're doing the curriculum statement for Wales'. And if you try to un-pick that a little more what they actually say is, 'What we do is educative, participative, creative and empowering'. And by repeating that mantra they actually frighten away the devils who really want to investigate what they are doing. And generally, that's the end of the conversation. There's no more after that ... Youth work is about working from that particular value base which is in itself a problem because firstly, we have difficulties in the articulation of those values and secondly, for many people ... they don't know that those values exist ...*

And actually having an opportunity to explore, challenge, question, debate, to analyse the value base of youth work is something that they have never had the opportunity to do.

'Disciplined discussion' is needed in youth worker training and development because, as Aristotle noted, the 'fundamental moral and intellectual activities that go to make up a flourishing life cannot be continuously engaged in with pleasure and interest unless they are engaged in as part of shared activities with others who are themselves morally good persons' (cited in Cooper, 1980: 331).

We live here and draw our strength from being a part of this community. We are known in the community and in holding true to our values we have earned the respect accorded to those who genuinely care about the neighbourhood and its people.

'Philosophy and the habit' are needed because wisdom brings virtue and virtue brings happiness (Socrates).

It's about honesty. If I can't be honest in the work relationship, if I have to suppress myself then I don't want to be involved in it. For me, it's as much about me as it is about the work because I like to feel that my work is an expression of me. It's my creativity and I have integrity within that. So I don't want to be involved in something that's going to diminish my integrity. Just doing something for the sake of doing it isn't part of my value system.

Virtue is needed because it is our human responsibility – 'The only worthwhile thing a person can do is to become as good a person as possible' (Confucius).

Youth work is about making a human to human connection with young people and that adds a kind of spiritual dimension to the relationship. By this I mean a deep appreciation of humanness – of human beings contacting each other in a way that isn't based on who the other person is – just based on the fact that they are human and no other criteria; that the person has intrinsic value because they are another human being on the planet. That's not easy, but I think it can be taught given reasonable raw material – that is a worker who has some spiritual sense or value base of their own.

In the process youth workers will need to:

- Overcome their selfishness.
- Gain an awareness of the roots of their fears (of life or uncertainty), their sense of powerlessness, distrust of people 'and the many other subtle roots that have grown together so thickly that it often is impossible to uproot them'.
- Change their practice.

- 'Go out of themselves' into the world outside of their own egos. (Fromm, 1993: 119)

For in the end, true knowledge of oneself and others is liberating and conducive to well-being (Fromm, 1993: 86).

Summary

This chapter identifies the skills and dispositions needed by youth workers, and the implications of this for their training and development. In so doing, it reiterates the importance of group work and communication skills and the ability to support young people through the experiential learning cycle.

However, developing effective youth work practice is not simply about accumulating a comprehensive set of skills, nor is it about the personal characteristics of the worker. Effective practice rests on the youth worker's values. This is because youth workers' values impact directly on their work and create the foundation for young people's moral reflections. Youth workers, therefore, need to develop ethical and reflective practice, not in the sense of adhering to a 'code of ethics', but rather, as a way of interpreting and giving meaning to the concepts and values involved in youth work.

Also, since reflection and discussions about principles and values are not merely intellectual exercises but should lead to action, the challenge for youth worker training and professional development is how to support workers to develop their 'philosophy' in terms of a clear set of values (understanding of virtue) and the 'habit' (disposition towards acting virtuously).

The proposition here is that 'philosophy and the habit' can be developed through participation in 'disciplined discussion' involving:

1. Serious discussion about values including getting people to see what it is like to live according to various value judgements.
2. Promotion of sensitivity to others and the consequences of one's actions.
3. Discussion of moral rules and principles – e.g. respect for persons.

Such an approach would require a structured supervision process based on learning from experience and providing opportunities for workers to:

- Develop their skills in critical thinking.
- Engage in disciplined discussion about values and moral principles.
- Develop the practise of virtue through action, reflection and learning.

The critical importance of this for youth work arises from the necessity for youth workers to be, themselves, well versed in the reflective and deliberative processes through which they seek to support young people.

Chapter 5

The future for youth work

This book argues that youth work is a distinct activity in its own right. An activity that is different from other forms of work with young people – not because of its methods, curriculum or target groups, but because of its core purpose, and arising from this, the particular kind of relationships that youth workers have with young people.

But youth work does not take place in a vacuum, and the agenda emerging for young people during the late 1990s increasingly reflected government concerns about:

- Young people aged 13–19.
- Young people not in education, employment or training.
- Young mothers.
- Young people engaged in or at risk of drug, alcohol or substance abuse.
- Young people engaged in or at risk of offending or anti-social behaviour.

In the process, youth work was *transformed* in order to help the government 'drive forward the range of policies impacting on young people, particularly the Connexions Service' (DfEE, 2001: 21). Consequently, *Transforming Youth Work: Developing Youth Work for Young People* (DfEE, 2001) proposed a range of roles for youth workers and youth services that highlighted their contribution to:

- The development of preventative strategies for enabling young people to make informed choices about avoiding crime, protection from drug or alcohol related dangers, preventing teenage pregnancy, healthy eating and living, achieving qualifications, securing employment, being valued and respected, contributing to the local community, taking full advantage of entitlements in a fair society, having access to a range of leisure time pursuits.
- Offering young people the chance to benefit from community and voluntary service (e.g. through Millennium Volunteers).
- Encouraging understanding and supporting the participation of groups experiencing discrimination.
- Developing relationships with young people 'at risk' so that they can intervene and prevent problems for young people in relation to drugs awareness, health issues, education, employment, accommodation.

- Providing a 'lifeline' for young people to joined-up support across local support agencies including social services, housing and the police.
- Contributing to strategies to prevent teenage pregnancy.
- Assisting in the development of participative and democratic models for young people to 'have a voice' in all aspects of the Connexions Service including design, delivery and governance; and wider (e.g. local youth councils, UK Youth Parliament, representation on local authority and community decision-making bodies).
- Becoming Personal Advisers.
- Contributing to the multi-disciplinary Connexions teams. (DfEE, 2001: 14–17)

One year later *Transforming Youth Work: Resourcing Excellent Youth Services* (DfES, 2002) described youth work as offering young people:

> . . . *particular ways of learning, characterised by processes which encourage personal and social development and reflect wider social issues. Young people can develop the skills and knowledge needed for their longer-term employability, including basic skills in literacy and numeracy, and an increased awareness of health and social issues, such as drugs and alcohol education.*

(DfES, 2002: 11)

Resourcing Excellent Youth Services (REYS) required that each local authority youth service develop a curriculum framework; and also identified annual youth service targets relating to:

- The level of 'reach' into the resident 13–19 population.
- The level of participation of the 13–19 population in youth work.
- The proportion of participants in youth work who gain recorded outcomes.
- The proportion of participants in youth work who gain accredited outcomes.
- Locally agreed targets for those young people assessed as not in education, employment or training (NEET) or who are at risk of, or who already fall into the categories; teenage pregnancy, drugs, alcohol or substance abuse or offending. (DfES, 2002: 16)

The 'commodification' of youth work

In response, Smith suggested that youth work within local authority youth services was being transformed not into something excellent but 'into something that is less than excellent and not youth work' (2003a: 15), and he identified six elements of the REYS specification which raised issues for youth services, youth workers and youth work.

- Centralisation: The requirement to address centrally defined targets, augmented by an increased emphasis on central monitoring represented, according to Smith, a shift in power to the centre in the governance of youth services, the impact of which would affect the 'degree of freedom that state-employed and state-funded youth workers have to respond to the needs and wishes of the young people they encounter' (Smith, 2003b: 2).
- Targeting: REYS identification of specific target groups had the potential to lead to a narrowing of the diversity of young people worked with, a focus on 'at risk' young people which could lead to stigmatisation and a shift of resources away from 'social capital building towards a more individualised social pathology' (2003b: 2).
- The focus on accreditation: Dramatically altered the focus of youth work and 'undermines the informal and convivial nature of youth work' (Smith, 2003b: 3). Smith's conclusion was that workers would feel under pressure to pursue activities that have obvious outcomes rather than trusting in the benefits of building relationships.
- Delivery rather than relationship: Organising work around concepts like outcome, curriculum and issue means there is a danger of overlooking what lies at the heart of youth work. Primarily, workers face losing 'relationship' as a defining feature of their practice (2003b: 3).
- Individualisation: Interventions targeted at individuals (e.g. within the Safer Cities Initiative, learning mentors, Connexions personal advisers) and an orientation towards individual achievements and benefits could result in 'a sharpening orientation to young people as individual consumers of a service rather than the creators of groups and activities' (2003b: 4).
- Bureaucratisation: In the form of 'joined-up' thinking, record-keeping and the surveillance and control of individuals (2003b: 5).

Smith's concern was that youth work was being 'commodified' in the sense that a heavy emphasis on the achievement of outcomes leads learning to be increasingly perceived as a commodity or investment, 'rather than as a way of exploring what might make for the good life of human flourishing.'

However, these elements of centralisation, targeting, bureaucratisation and so on, have become evident not only in relation to the youth service's work with young people but also more broadly as Pitts observed:

Since 1997, along with concerns about their educational attainment and employability, the likelihood of lower class children and young people drifting into crime and disorder has been a major area of governmental concern, and these concerns have spawned a plethora of new initiatives. A study undertaken in 2002/3 (Crimmens et al., 2004) found that street-based youth work had expanded significantly since the election of New

Labour in 1997, as a direct result of these new initiatives . . . However, whereas in the past, street-based youth work had tended to offer a broad-based 'social education' to the generality of young people in disadvantaged neighbourhoods, the projects surveyed in 2002/3 were far more likely to be targeting young people involved in crime and disorder, drug use, truancy and excluded from school.

(Pitts, 2004: 10)

Such developments have increasingly involved:

- The utilisation of methods and approaches, which had been consistently developed within youth work (e.g. group work, detached work).
- The recruitment of youth workers to pursue, through their relationships with young people, the objectives of the initiatives resulting from central-ised policy imperatives which focused especially on work related to crime prevention, health promotion, and particularly, work with young people termed 'disaffected' and 'socially excluded'. (Piper and Piper, 1998)

The effect on youth work was twofold. Firstly, a growing range of practitioners increasingly laid claim to being involved in supporting young people's personal development. This included, for example, Connexions personal advisers, learning mentors, youth justice workers such as those working for Youth Offending Teams and Youth Inclusion Programmes, drug action workers and those working on projects to tackle teenage pregnancy. (Young, 1998a; 1998b: Jeffs and Smith, 1992; 2002)

Secondly, youth work became increasingly targeted towards the groups of young people identified as priorities by different 'external' funders – e.g. Lottery, European Social Fund, special government funding schemes etc (Marken, Perrett and Wylie, 1998).

The message from government became increasingly clear. Local authority youth services needed to meet two conditions:

- Focus their efforts much more (perhaps primarily) on those young people who were pre-defined as excluded, disaffected or disadvantaged; and (in order to do this effectively)
- Increasingly work in partnership with other youth-serving agencies. (Davies, 1999b)

However, partnership work provided not only opportunities for cross-agency planning and 'joined-up' responses to young people's needs, but also led to a blurring of the boundaries between youth work and other forms of work with young people. For example, in the context of youth justice work, Pitts observed:

The tendency of the youth justice system to annex other child and youth serving agencies has been evident since the 1980s (Pitts, 1988). However, from the late 1990s, as a result of the articulation of a far broader range of agencies and services, driven by changed funding regimes and facilitated by multi-agency working and the legal and scientific capacity to identify not only 'offending' populations but also young people who are 'anti-social', 'pre-delinquent' or 'at risk', the youth justice system in the 21st century has become a qualitative different entity. Just as the boundaries between children and young people who are 'offending', 'anti-social', 'pre-delinquent' and 'at risk' are being progressively blurred in policy and law, so the boundaries of youth justice, community safety, education, drugs services, social welfare and crime control are becoming ever more fluid, and ever more opaque.

(Pitts, 2004: 10)

Indeed, such a blurring of boundaries was to become highly 'fluid and opaque' as a result of the Children Bill (2004) which required local authorities and relevant agencies to form Children's Trusts as a mechanism for bringing services for children and young people together under one single organisation responsible for securing integrated commissioning leading to more 'joined up' service delivery for children, young people and families.

The 'Change for Children' agenda spearheaded through *Every Child Matters* (DfES, 2003) brought local authority youth services alongside other services in contributing to the achievement of the five ECM outcomes for children and young people aged 0–19 living in England:

- **Be healthy:** enjoying good physical and mental health and living a healthy lifestyle.
- **Stay safe:** being protected from harm and neglect.
- **Enjoy and achieve:** getting the most out of life and developing the skills for adulthood.
- **Make a positive contribution:** being involved with the community and society and not engaging in anti-social or offending behaviour.
- **Achieve economic well-being:** not being prevented by economic disadvantage from achieving their full potential in life.

Later, *Youth Matters* (DfES, 2005), which built on ECM in promoting the achievement of the five key outcomes for young people, addressed four key challenges:

- How to engage more young people in positive activities and empower them to shape the services they receive.
- How to encourage more young people to volunteer and become involved in their communities.
- How to provide better information, advice and guidance to young people to help them make informed choice about their lives.

- How to provide better and more personalised intensive support for each young person who has serious problems or gets into trouble.

These were welcomed developments in the provision of opportunities, challenge and support to young people. But, against a backdrop of policy and legislation aimed at curbing 'yobbish' and anti-social behaviour (e.g. Anti-Social Behaviour Orders introduced in the Crime and Disorder Act 1998; Dispersal Orders introduced in The Anti-Social Behaviour Act 2003); and a pervading discourse referred to by different commentators as 'youth *as* trouble or youth *in* trouble' (Griffin, 1997); youth as 'thugs, users and victims' (Jeffs and Smith, 1998); 'young people-as-moral underclass-in need of social integration' (Levitas, 1998); the danger was that 'Youth Matters' and the change for children agenda would distort youth work's sense of purpose. Transforming it from an activity concerned with the education and welfare of young people as *people*, and one in which young people (rather than, say, parents or even the 'community') are seen as 'the clientele' (Davies, 1991: 5); to an activity concerned with the training and welfare of young people as *workers and citizens*, and one in which society and central government are seen as the 'clientele'.

The future for youth work within local authorities would therefore rest on the extent to which local youth services were able to:

- Position themselves within local structures so as to support coordination and integration while ensuring the appropriate contribution of youth work and youth workers.
- Exert their influence through contributing to the policies and provision of other young people serving agencies and corporate policy and decision-making whilst retaining a clear sense of the purpose of youth work as opposed to other forms of work with young people.
- Raise the profile of young people through supporting young people led initiatives and lobbying for recognition of young people's needs and the contribution they make to their community/society.
- Increase the credibility of youth work through:
  - Providing clarity about the purpose of youth work and articulating this in terms that others can understand.
  - Promoting the strengths of youth work in meeting young people's personal and social development needs and supporting their contribution to their community/society.
  - Improving the quality of youth work practice, provision and management so as to make everyday youth work a truly profound and self-reflective practice.

In the meantime, voluntary youth organisations and others working with young people in the voluntary and community sector continue to utilise and build on the principles and practice that underpin effective youth work – for example projects involved in The National Youth Agency managed Neighbourhood Support Fund programme (Young, 2005).

The values and principles of the project workers are around youth work. It's not a teacher based kind of relationship. It's much more on a 1–to–1 level where young people are valued and where the emphasis is on finding young people's strengths, not focusing on their weaknesses and trying to fix them, although that happens. It's about promoting young people's strengths and supporting them, and recognising what they can do which helps them to re-motivate themselves.

The small groups and informal atmosphere means that the workers can really talk with the young people, take on board their issues and really understand them. They can come at things from the young person's perspective and really focus on what the young person needs. The relationship between the workers and young people is also very different from what the young people have probably been used to at school. The project workers are from a youth work background so they talk to young people at their level. They talk to them as human beings, as equals. They show the young people respect and young people show respect in return. They understand the issues that affect young people and take them into account. The young people can relate to that.

Actually, the youth service has always fully supported the project and it has always worked to the three principles of youth work – core values of youth work; experiential learning; and personal and social development.

(Young, 2005)

Reclaiming youth work

The argument proffered here represents an ideal for youth work – a statement of what youth work 'ought' to be. It is a universal truth claim in much the same way as other universal truth claims have been made about the values underpinning youth work (Davies, 1996; DfES, 2002), and the 'key dimensions' (Smith, 2002a) and 'defining features' that characterise youth work practice (Davies, 2005).

However, whilst such 'key dimensions' and 'defining features' are helpful in offering a comprehensive set of defining characteristics for practice, they do not explain the purpose of youth work, and therefore, the particular contribution that youth work makes to young people's lives. That unique and distinctive contribution, I maintain, can only be understood through a careful discernment of youth work's core purpose and underlying philosophy.

The proposition here is that the core purpose of youth work is to engage young people in *moral philosophising* through which they make sense of themselves, their experiences and their world.

This is based on voluntary *relationships* with young people that involve accepting and valuing young people, honesty, trust, respect and reciprocity. Through such relationships youth workers support, enable and inspire young people to:

- Engage in philosophical inquiry through 'conversation'.
- Learn from their experience.
- Cultivate virtuous expression through practise.

This *process* of reflection and self-examination supports young people to increasingly integrate their values, actions and identity, and take charge of themselves as empowered and authentic human beings.

In the process young people learn to explore their values, deliberate on the principles of their own moral judgements and make reasoned choices and informed decisions that can be sustained through committed action. They also develop:

- Skills in critical thinking and rational judgement.
- The ability to engage in 'moral inquiry' about what is 'good' and conducive to the 'good life' generally – i.e. the ability which Aristotle called the development of practical wisdom.
- A disposition towards virtue (adherence to moral and ethical standards) as a central feature of their identity and responsibility as social beings in a social world.

The implication for youth worker training and development is that workers need to be provided with the opportunity for their own self-exploration, the examination of their own values, the development of their own critical skills and the enlargement of their own capacity for moral philosophy. This is crucial, not only for their own personal development but also, and important-ly, in order to enable them to become well versed in the reflective and deliberative processes through which they seek to support young people.

The central assertion of this book is, therefore, that youth work is and always has been fundamentally concerned with the kind of people young people are, and will become.

Whether this comes from a dedication to their personal development, social and political education (HMSO, 1960; 1969; 1982), as emanating from 'traditions' in social and leisure provision, character-building, personal and social development, rescuing, welfaring or politicising (Smith, 1988); or from a commitment to the principles of education, participation, empowerment and equality of opportunity (National Youth Bureau, 1991).

Whether it seeks to prepare young people for the responsibilities, oppor-tunities and expectations of adulthood and citizenship (DfES, 2002); or serves the functions of socialisation, social change or social justice (Merton, 2004).

Whether it is a way of exploring what might make for human flourishing in the sense that 'excellent youth work involves living, working for, and inviting people to share, the good life' (Smith, 2003b: 11), or, as proposed here, a way of engaging young people in the process of moral philosophising through which they make sense of themselves and their world.

Whatever the underlying impetus youth work is fundamentally concerned with who young people are, and who they are to become *as people*.

Yet, as ever, and I believe this applies not only to spiritual teaching but also to all teaching, hearsay and folklore . . .

Never believe any spiritual teaching because it is repeatedly recited; or because it is written down in the scriptures; or because it has been handed down from teacher to disciple; nor because everybody around you believes it; nor because it has metaphysical qualities; nor because it agrees with what you believe anyway; nor because you can rationalise it. Don't believe it if it is a viewpoint which you need to defend and don't believe it because the teacher is a reputable person or because the teacher said so . . . Don't believe something because it's a tradition, or because everybody around you does it, or because it's written in a book, but only, the Buddha said, if you have inquired into it and found it to be useful and true.

(Khema, 1987: 160)

References

Aristotle (384–322 BC) *The Nicomachean Ethics*. translated by Welldon, J. (1987) Buffalo, NY: Promethus Books.

Bandura, A. (1974) (Ed.) *Psychological Modelling: Conflicting Theories*. New York: Lieber-Atherton.

Banks, S. (1997) The Dilemmas of Intervention, in Roche, J. and Tucker, S. (Eds.) (1997) *Youth in Society*. London: Sage.

Banks, S. (1999) (Ed.) *Ethical Issues in Youth Work*. London: Routledge.

Barrow, R. (1975) *Moral Philosophy for Education*. London: Allen & Unwin Ltd.

Barrow, R. (1981) *The Philosophy of Schooling*. Brighton: Wheatsheaf Books Ltd.

Becsky, S. and Perrett, J. (1999) *Youth Policy and Youth Services in the United Kingdom*. Leicester: IJAB/NYA.

Benn, S. and Peters, R. (1959) *Social Principles and the Democratic State*. London: Allen & Unwin

Bentham, J. (1748–1832) *Introduction to the Principles of Morals and Legislation*. (1948) Oxford: Basil Blackwell.

Berger, P. and Luckman, T. (1967) *The Social Construction of Reality*. Harmondsworth: Penguin.

Board of Education (1939) *In the Service of Youth (Circular 1486)*. London: HMSO (now available in *Documents of Historical Importance*. 1982, National Youth Bureau).

Board of Education (1940) *The Challenge of Youth (Circular 1516)* London: HMSO (now available in *Documents of Historical Importance*. 1982, National Youth Bureau).

Booton, F. (1985) *Studies in Social Education: Vol. 1 1860–1890*. Hove: Benfield Press.

Brabeck, M. (1993) Moral Judgment: Theory and Research on Differences between Males and Females, in Larrabee M.J. (Ed.) *An Ethic of Care*. London: Routledge

Brew, J. Macalister (1943) *In The Service of Youth*. London: Faber and Faber.

Brew, J. Macalister (1957) *Youth and Youth Groups*. London: Faber and Faber.

Brookfield, S. (1987) *Developing Critical Thinking*. Milton Keynes: Open University Press.

Bruner, J. (1990) *Acts of Meaning*. Cambridge MA: Harvard University Press.

Burke, T. and Loewenstein, P. (1998) Me and my Shadow. *Young People Now*, Issue 107, March 1998: 32–3.

Carpenter, V. and Young, K. (1986) *Coming In From the Margins – Youth Work with Girls and Young Women*. Leicester: National Association of Youth Clubs.

Clutterbuck, D. and Sweeney, J. (1997) *Coaching and Mentoring*. London: Clutterbuck Palmer Schneider Ltd.

Coleman, J. (1992) The Nature of Adolescence, in Coleman, J. and Warren-Adamson, C. (Eds.) (1992) *Youth Policy in the 1990s: The Way Forward*. London: Routledge.

Coleman, J., Catan, L. and Dennison, C. (1997) You're the Last Person I'd Talk To, in Roche, J. and Tucker, S. (Eds.) (1997) *Youth in Society*. London: Sage.

Coleman, J. and Hendry, L. (1999) *The Nature of Adolescence*, 3rd Edition. London: Routledge.

Confucius (551–479 BC) *The Analects*, translated by Lau, D.C. (1979) Harmondsworth: Penguin.

Cooper, J. (1980) Aristotle on Friendship, in Rorty, A. (Ed.) *Essays on Aristotle's Ethics*. Los Angeles: University of California Press.

Cortazzi, M. (1993) *Narrative Analysis*. London: The Falmer Press.

Crimmens, D. and Whalen, A. (1999) Rights Based Approaches to Work with Young People, in Banks, S. (Ed.) *Ethical Issues in Youth Work*. London: Routledge.

Crimmens, D., Factor, F., Jeffs, T., Pitts, J., Pugh, C., Spence, J. and Turner, P. (2004) *Reaching Socially Excluded Young People*. Leicester: JRF/National Youth Agency.

Crossley, M. (2000) *Introducing Narrative Psychology: Self, Trauma and the Construction of Meaning*. Buckingham: Open University Press.

Davies, B. and Gibson, A. (1967) *The Social Education of the Adolescent*. London: University of London Press.

Davies, B. (1991) Whose Youth Service Curriculum? *Youth and Policy*, March 1991, 32: 1–9.

Davies, B. (1996) Values in Youth Work. *Young People Now*, August 1996, Issue 88.

Davies, B. (1999a) *From Voluntaryism to Welfare State*. Leicester: Youth Work Press.

Davies, B. (1999b) *From Thatcherism to New Labour*. Leicester: Youth Work Press.

Davies, B. (2005) Youth Work: A Manifesto for Our Times. *Youth and Policy*, Summer 2005, Issue 88: 5–27.

De Silva, P. (1993) Buddhist Ethics, in Singer, P. (Ed.) *A Companion to Ethics.* Oxford: Blackwell.

Dewey, J. (1961) *Democracy and Education: An Introduction to the Philosophy of Education.* New York: Macmillan.

DfEE (2001) *Transforming Youth Work: Developing Youth Work for Young People.* London: DfEE.

DfES (2002) *Transforming Youth Work: Resourcing Excellent Youth Services.* London: DfES.

DfES (2003) *Every Child Matters.* London: The Stationery Office.

DfES (2005) *Youth Matters.* London: The Stationery Office.

Eggleston, J. (1976) *Adolescence and Community: The Youth Service in Britain.* London: Edward Arnold.

Erikson, H. (1968) *Identity: Youth and Crisis.* London: Faber.

Ennis, R. (1962) A Concept of Critical Thinking: A Proposed Basis for Research in the Teaching and Evaluation of Critical Thinking Ability. *Harvard Educational Review*, 32: 1, 81–111.

Everitt, A. Hardiker, P. Littlewood, J. and Mullender, A. (1992) *Applied Research for Better Practice.* London: Macmillan.

Fisher, A. (1991) Critical Thinking, in Coles, M. and Robinson, W. (Eds.) *Teaching Thinking.* Bristol: Bristol Classical Press.

Foucault, M. (1988) Technologies of the Self, in Martin, L., Gutman, H. and Hutton, P. (Eds.) *Technologies of the Self: A Seminar with Michel Foucault.* Amherst, University of Massachusetts Press.

Franklin, A. and Franklin, B. (1990) Age and Power, in Jeffs, T. and Smith, M. (Eds.) *Young People, Inequality and Youth Work.* London: Macmillan.

Freire, P. (1976) *Education: The Practice of Freedom.* London: Writers and Readers Publishing Cooperative.

Fromm, E. (1993) *The Art of Being.* London: Constable.

Giddens, A. (1991) *Modernity and Self Identity.* Cambridge: Polity Press.

Gilligan, C. (1982) *In a Different Voice.* Cambridge MA: Harvard University Press.

Gramsci, A. (1971) *Selections from Prison Notebooks.* (Trans. and Ed. by Hoare, Q. and Smith, G.) London: Lawrence Wishart.

Green, M. and Christian, C. (1998) *Accompanying Young People on the Spiritual Path.* London: The National Society/Church House Publishing.

Griffin, C. (1993) *Representations of Youth: The Study of Youth and Adolescence in Britain and America.* Cambridge: Polity Press.

Griffin, C. (1997) Representations of the Young, in Roche, J. and Tucker, S. (Eds.) *Youth in Society,* London: Sage.

HMSO (1944) *Teachers and Youth Leaders: Report of the Committee appointed by the Board of Education to Consider the Supply, Recruitment and Training of Teachers and Youth Leaders.* (The McNair Report).

HMSO (1960) *The Youth Service in England and Wales.* The Albemarle Committee.

HMSO (1969) *Youth and Community Work in the 70s.* Milson-Fairbairn Committees.

HMSO (1982) *Experience and Participation.* Thompson Committee.

Hume, D. (1738) *Treatise of Human Nature.* Selby-Bigge, L. and Nidditch, P. (Eds.) (1978) Oxford: Clarendon Press.

Jeffs, T. and Smith, M. (1992) Putting Youth Work in its Place. *Youth and Policy,* 36, March 1992, 10–16.

Jeffs, T. and Smith, M. (1998) The Problem of 'Youth' for Youth Work. *Youth and Policy,* 62, Winter 1998/99, 45–66.

Jeffs, T. and Smith, M. (1999a) *Informal Education: Conversation, Democracy and Learning* 2nd edn. Derby: Education Now Publishing Co-operative.

Jeffs, T. and Smith, M. (1999b) Resourcing Youth Work: Dirty Hands and Tainted Money, in Banks, S. (Ed.) *Ethical Issues in Youth Work.* London: Routledge.

Jeffs, T. and Smith, M. (2002) Individualisation and Youth Work. *Youth and Policy,* 76, Summer 2002 39–65.

Kant, I. (1785) *Groundwork of the Metaphysics of Morals.* Translated by Paton, H.J. (1948) *The Moral Law.* NY: Harper Torchbooks.

Kellner, M. (1993) Jewish Ethics, in Singer, P. (Ed.) *A Companion To Ethics.* Oxford: Blackwell.

Khema, A. (1987) *Being Nobody, Going Nowhere.* London: Wisdom Publications.

King George's Jubilee Trust (1951) *Youth Service Tomorrow* – A report of a meeting arranged by King George's Jubilee Trust and held at Ashridge, 27–30 April 1951.

Kleinig, J. (1982) *Philosophical Issues in Education.* London: Croom Helm.

Kohlberg, L. (1981) *Essays on Moral Development: Vol I The Philosophy of Moral Development.* San Francisco, Calif: Harper and Row.

Kohlberg, L. (1983) *Essays on Moral Development: Vol II The Psychology of Moral Development.* San Francisco, Calif: Harper and Row.

Kolb, D. (1984) *Experiential Learning.* Englewood Cliffs, N.Y: Prentice-Hall.

Kosman, L.A. (1980) Being Properly Affected: Virtues and Feelings in Aristotle's Ethics, in Rorty, A. (Ed.) *Essays on Aristotle's Ethics.* Berkeley: University of California Press.

Kupperman, J. (1983) *The Foundations of Morality.* London: Allen & Unwin.

Leighton, J. (1972) *The Principles and Practice of Youth and Community Work.* London: Chester House Publications.

Levitas, R. (1998) *The Inclusive Society? – Social Exclusion and New Labour.* London: Macmillan.

Lipman, M. (1988) *Philosophy Goes to School.* Philadelphia: Temple University Press.

Lorenz, W. (1996) Pedagogical Principles for Anti-racist Strategies, in Aluffi-Pentini, A. and Lorenz, W. (Eds.) *Anti-Racist Work with Young People.* Lyme Regis: Russell House Publishing.

Marken, M., Perrett, P. and Wylie, T. (1998) *England's Youth Service – the 1998 Audit.* Leicester: Youth Work Press.

Marshak, R. (1998) A Discourse on Discourse: Redeeming the Meaning of Talk, in Grant, D., Keenoy, T. and Oswick, C. (Eds.) (1998) *Discourse and Organisation.* London: Sage.

McAdams, D. (1993) *The Stories we Live by: Personal Myths and the Making of the Self.* New York: Morrow.

Mencius – [The] *Mencius,* translated by Lau, D.C. (1970) Harmondsworth: Penguin. (Mencius was probably born a century or so after the death of Confucius and likely to have died by the end of the fourth century BC. The 'Mencius' was written in the years just after 320 BC)

Merton, B. (2004) *Evaluation of the Impact of Youth Work.* London: DfES.

Merton, B. and Wylie, T. (2002) *Towards a Contemporary Curriculum for Youth Work.* Leicester: NYA.

Midgley, M. (1997) Can Education Be Moral?, in Smith, R. and Standish, P. (Eds.) (1997) *Teaching Right and Wrong: Moral Education in the Balance.* Stoke on Trent: Trentham Books.

Milson, F. (1970) *Youth Work in the 1970s.* London: Routledge and Kegan Paul.

Ministry of Education (1945) *The Purpose and Content of the Youth Service: A Report of the Youth Advisory Council appointed by the Minister of Education in 1943.* London: HMSO.

Morgan, S. and Banks, S. (1999) The Youth Worker as Confidant, in Banks, S. (Ed.) *Ethical Issues in Youth Work.* London: Routledge.

Morrow, V. and Richards, M. (1996) *Transition to Adulthood.* York: Joseph Rowntree Foundation.

Nanji, A. (1993) Islamic Ethics, in Singer, P. (Ed.) *A Companion to Ethics.* Oxford: Blackwell.

National Youth Agency (1997) *Mentoring* - briefing paper, November 1997.

National Youth Agency (2001) *Ethical Conduct in Youth Work: A Statement of Values and Principles from the National Youth Agency.*

National Youth Agency (2003) *NYA Guide to Youth Work and Youth Services.*

National Youth Bureau (1990) *Danger or Opportunity: Towards a Core Curriculum for the Youth Service?*

National Youth Bureau (1991) *Towards a Core Curriculum – The Next Step: Report of the Second Ministerial Conference.*

Paulo NTO (January 2002) *National Occupational Standards for Youth Work in the UK.,* www.paulo.org.uk

Philip, K. and Hendry, L. (1996) Young People and Mentoring – Towards a Typology? *Journal of Adolescence.* Issue 19, 189–201.

Piaget, J. (1932) *The Moral Judgment of the Child.* London: Routledge and Kegan Paul.

Pini, M. (1997) Technologies of the Self, in Roche, J. and Tucker, S. (Eds.) *Youth in Society.* London: Sage.

Piper, H. and Piper, J. (1998) Disaffected Youth – A Wicked Issue: A Worse Label. *Youth and Policy,* No 62. Winter 1998/99, 32–43.

Pitts, J. (1988) *The Politics of Juvenile Crime.* London: Sage.

Pitts, J. (2004) The Recent History of Youth Justice in England and Wales, in Bateman, T. and Pitts, J. (Eds.) *The RHP Companion to Youth Justice.* Lyme Regis: Russell House Publishing.

Plato (c 427–347 BC) *The Dialogues of Plato:* Vol 2 The Symposium and Other Dialogues, translated by Jowett, B. (1970) London: Sphere Books Limited.

Preston, R. (1993) Christian Ethics, in Singer, P. (Ed.) *A Companion to Ethics.* Oxford: Basil Blackwell Ltd.

Pring, R. (1984) *Personal and Social Education in the Curriculum.* London: Hodder and Stoughton.

Richardson, J. (1997) The Path to Adulthood and the Failure of Youth Work, in Ledgerwood, I. and Kendra, N. (Eds.) *The Challenge of the Future.* Lyme Regis: Russell House Publishing.

Riessman, C. (1993) *Narrative Analysis.* Newbury Park, Calif: Sage.

Robinson, L. (1997) Black Adolescent Identity and the Inadequacies of Western Psychology, in Roche, J. and Tucker, S. (Eds.) *Youth in Society.* London: Sage.

Rokeach, M. (1973) *The Nature of Human Values.* New York: Free Press.

Rorty, A. (1993) Moral Imperialism versus Moral Conflict: Conflicting Aims of Education, in Darling-Smith, B. (Ed.) *Can Virtue Be Taught?* Notre Dame: University of Notre Dame Press.

Schneewind, J. (1993) Modern Moral Philosophy, in Singer, P. (Ed.) *A Companion to Ethics.* Oxford: Basil Blackwell Ltd.

Shotter, J. (1993) *Conversational Realities: Constructing Life through Language.* London: Sage.

Singer, P. (1997) *How are we to live?* Oxford: Oxford University Press.

Smith, D. (1987) *Reshaping the Youth Service,* Leicester: National Youth Bureau.

Smith, M. (1988) *Developing Youth Work.* Milton Keynes: Open University Press.

Smith, Mark K. (2002a, 1999) *Introducing the Theory and Practice of Youth Work,* www.infed.org

Smith, M. (2003a) The End of Youth Work? *Young People Now.* 5–11 February 2003, 15.

Smith, M. (2003b) From Youth Work to Youth Development. The new Government Framework for English Youth Services. *Youth and Policy 79.*

Available in the informal education archives: www.infed.org/archives/jeffs_ and_smith/smith_youth_work_to_youth_development.htm

Social Exclusion Unit (2000) *National Strategy for Neighbourhood Renewal: Report of Policy Action Team 12: Young People.*

Streng, F. (1993) Cultivating Virtue in a Religiously Plural World: Possibilities and Problems, in Darling-Smith, B. (Ed.) *Can Virtue Be Taught?* Notre Dame: University of Notre Dame Press.

Taylor, C. (1989) *Sources of the Self: The Making of Modern Identity,* Cambridge: Cambridge University Press.

Thompson, N. (1997) *Anti-Discriminatory Practice.* London: Macmillan.

Wallemacq, A. and Sims, D. (1998) The Struggle with Sense, in Grant, D., Keenoy, T. and Oswick, C. (Eds.) *Discourse and Organisation.* London: Sage.

Weick, K. (1995) *Sensemaking in Organisations.* London: Sage Publications.

Whalley, M. (1991) Philosophy for Children, in Coles, M. and Robinson, W. (Eds.) *Teaching Thinking*, Bristol: Bristol Classical Press.

Williams, B. (1993) *Ethics and the Limits of Philosophy.* Hammersmith: Fontana Press.

Williamson, B. (1997) Moral Learning: a Lifelong Task, in Smith, R. and Standish, P. (Eds.) *Teaching Right And Wrong: Moral Education in the Balance.* Stoke on Trent: Trentham Books.

Woods, C. (1995) *State of the Queer Nation.* London: Cassell.

Wylie, T. (1998) A Domesday Book of Today's Youth Service. *Young People Now.* November 1998, 24–5.

Wyn, J. and White, R. (1997) *Rethinking Youth.* London: Sage.

Young Men's Christian Association (1844) *The YMCA in Focus.* 1987.

Young, K. (1998a) A Different Agenda? *Young People Now.* Issue 109, May 1998 34–5.

Young, K. (1998b) Sticking to the Knitting *Youth and Policy* No 60, Summer 1998, 84–9.

Young, K. (1999) The Youth Worker as Guide, Philosopher and Friend, in Banks, S. (Ed.) *Ethical Issues in Youth Work*, London: Routledge.

Young, K. (2005) *People with Potential, not people with problems – an evaluation of voluntary sector projects working with disengaged young people*, Leicester: National Youth Agency.